THOMAS LININGER

Sedona, AZ Travel Guide 2024

Discovering Arizona's secrets from Cathedral Rock to Mii Amo Spa, a Multifaceted Escape

Contents

Disclaimer

The goal of this book is to provide you with valuable information about the place you are going.

However, it does not contain images or maps.

I strongly advise that you conduct your own research before embarking on your trip. There are online tools available to help you plan and enjoy your journey.

Keep in mind that this travel guide is a comprehensive resource, but it is essential to explore the places you want to visit in detail before you lea ve.

Introduction

A Journey Through Time: The Layers of Sedona's History

Sedona's story stretches far beyond its recent popularity as a tourist destination.

Ancient Dwellings:

- The land cradled Native American settlements for millennia. The Sinagua, Hohokam, and Anasazi tribes farmed, hunted, and built cliff dwellings, leaving behind a legacy of resilience in a harsh environment.
- **Impact on Present Day:** These ancient dwellings, like those at Montezuma Castle National Monument (outside Sedona), inspire awe and spark curiosity about the region's early inhabitants. The Sedona Heritage Museum showcases artifacts and explains their way of life.

European Arrival (1583):

- Spanish conquistadors searching for gold were the first Europeans to set foot in the area. Their impact was minimal, leaving the land largely untouched.

Settlers and Ranchers (1876 Onwards):

- John J. Thompson, in 1876, became the first Anglo settler, drawn by the fertile Oak Creek Canyon for farming. More homesteaders followed, establishing ranches and orchards.
- **Key Historical Figure:** Theodore Carlton Schnebly, the first postmaster, named the town Sedona after his wife in 1902.

The Tourist Boom (1950s Onwards):

- The mid-20th century saw a shift towards tourism. Sedona's breathtaking red rock formations, coupled with its reputation as a spiritual vortex, attracted visitors seeking natural beauty and renewal.

Impact of History on Sedona Today:

- Sedona's charm lies in the unique blend of its natural wonders and its human history.
- **Historical Sites and Museums:** The Sedona Heritage Museum offers a window into the lives of early settlers and Native Americans. Slide Rock State Park preserves the remnants of Pendley's irrigation system, a testament to the ingenuity of early farmers.

Landmarks and Activities:

- **Chapel of the Holy Cross:** Built into a butte in 1956, this chapel blends mid-century architecture with the red rock landscape.
- **Jeep Tours:** Explore ancient petroglyphs and hidden canyons, learning about the region's geological and cultural heritage.

Geographic and Climatic Gem

Sedona's beauty is a result of its unique location and climate.

Absolute and Relative Location:

- **Latitude & Longitude:** Sedona sits at approximately 34°53' N latitude and 111°48' W longitude
- **Relative Location:** Nestled in Yavapai County, Arizona, Sedona is:
- 115 miles north of Phoenix, the state capital [Distance from Sedona, AZ to Phoenix, AZ].
- Adjacent to the Coconino National Forest to the west.
- In close proximity to the dramatic Oak Creek Canyon, a popular scenic destination.

Physical Characteristics:

- **Landforms:** Sedona's defining feature is its stunning red rock formations, primarily composed of sandstone and shale shaped by millions of years of erosion. These formations include iconic landmarks like Chimney Rock, Courthouse Butte, and Bell Rock.
- **Water Bodies:** While not abundant, Sedona features Oak Creek, a permanent stream that carves through the canyon, offering a vibrant contrast to the red rocks
- **Natural Resources:** The primary natural resource is the breathtaking landscape itself, attracting tourism and recreation. Additionally, the region holds potential for copper mining, although currently inactive.

Climate:

- **Climate Zone:** Sedona falls within a temperate semi-arid climate zone. This translates to warm, dry summers and mild winters with occasional snowfall.

Weather Patterns:

- **Summer (June - August):** Hottest and driest months. Average highs reach 97°F (34°C) with lows around 64°F (17°C). Afternoon thunderstorms are common, bringing temporary relief from the heat.
- **Spring (March - May) & Fall (September - November):** Pleasant seasons with comfortable temperatures. Average highs range from 77°F (25°C) to 88°F (31°C) with lows dropping to 40°F (4°C) at night. Spring can see occasional rain showers.
- **Winter (December - February):** Mildest season with the lowest chance of precipitation. Average highs hover around 57°F (14°C) with lows dipping to 31°F (-1°C). Snowfall is infrequent but can occur.

Seasonal Variations:

- Rainfall is concentrated in the winter months (around 7 inches annually), with minimal precipitation throughout the rest of the year. This creates a stark contrast between the lush vegetation along Oak Creek and the arid red rock landscape.
- **Hiking:** Spring and fall offer ideal hiking conditions with comfortable temperatures. Summer heat can be challenging, while winter nights can be chilly at higher elevations.

Planning your Trip

Sedona Travel Essentials

Here's a comprehensive list of travel essentials to ensure a smooth and enjoyable trip to Sedona:

Documentation:

- **Valid Passport (if required):** While most visitors won't need a visa for Sedona (refer to previous information on visas), a valid passport is required for citizens of countries outside the U.S. visa waiver program. Check the U.S. Department of State website for details (https://travel.state.gov/content/travel/en/us-visas/tourism-visit/visa-waiver-program.html).
- **ESTA (if applicable):** Even with a visa waiver program country passport, you may need an Electronic System for Travel Authorization (ESTA) to enter the United States. Apply online at https://esta.cbp.dhs.gov/.
- **Travel Insurance (optional):** Consider travel insurance for peace of mind, covering potential trip cancellations, medical emergencies, or lost luggage.
- **Driver's License (if renting a car):** A valid driver's license from your home country is required to rent a car in the United States. An International Driving Permit (IDP) is recommended but not mandatory.

You won't need a visa to visit Sedona, Arizona, USA! Here's why:

- **Sedona is located within the United States:** The United States has a visa waiver program for citizens of many countries. This means that if you're a citizen of a country participating in the program, you generally don't need a visa for stays less than 90 days.

Who Might Need a Visa:

- Travelers who are not citizens of a visa waiver program country will need a visa to enter the United States. You can find a list of participating countries on the U.S. Department of State travel website https://trave l.state.gov/content/travel/en/us-visas/tourism-visit/visa-waiver-prog ram.html.

If You Do Need a Visa:

- The process for obtaining a visa can vary depending on your nationality and the purpose of your visit. In most cases, you'll need to apply at a U.S. embassy or consulate in your home country.
- The U.S. Department of State website https://travel.state.gov/content/ travel/en/us-visas/tourism-visit/visa-waiver-program.html provides information on visa types, application procedures, and required documents.

Documents Typically Required for a U.S. Visa:

- A valid passport
- A completed visa application form
- A passport-sized photograph
- Proof of travel arrangements (roundtrip flight tickets)
- Proof of sufficient funds to support your stay in the U.S.
- In some cases, additional documentation may be required, such as a letter

of invitation or proof of employment.

Important to Remember:

- Visa processing times can vary, so it's important to apply well in advance of your trip, especially if you need to schedule an interview at a U.S. embassy or consulate.
- Even if you are a citizen of a visa waiver program country, you may still need to apply for an Electronic System for Travel Authorization (ESTA) before traveling to the United States. You can apply for ESTA online at https://esta.cbp.dhs.gov/.

Currency:

- **The United States Dollar (USD) is the official currency in Sedona.** Carry cash for smaller purchases, entrance fees at some attractions, or gratuities, but many places accept credit cards.
- **Currency Exchange:** If you're traveling from outside the U.S., exchange some currency to USD before your trip or use ATMs upon arrival. Be aware of potential exchange rates and fees.

General Packing List for Sedona:

Clothing:

- **Layers:** Consider the season and pack accordingly.
- **Base Layers:** Moisture-wicking shirts and quick-drying pants for comfort during hikes or outdoor activities.
- **Mid Layers:** Fleece jackets, sweaters, or light jackets for cooler evenings or layering.

- **Outerwear:** A windproof or rain jacket for potential weather changes, especially during spring and fall.
- **Hiking Clothes:** Sturdy hiking pants or convertible hiking pants, comfortable hiking shirts.
- **Casual wear:** Comfortable clothing for exploring towns, relaxing at your accommodation, or enjoying meals.
- **Swimsuit (optional):** For swimming in Oak Creek or enjoying a resort pool (check regulations for designated swimming areas).
- **Underwear and Socks:** Pack enough for the duration of your trip. Consider quick-drying and moisture-wicking options for comfort.
- **Hats:** A wide-brimmed hat for sun protection and a warmer hat for cooler evenings (optional).

Accessories:

- **Sunglasses:** Essential for year-round sun protection.
- **Sunscreen (SPF 30 or higher):** Protect your skin from the strong Arizona sun.
- **Scarf (optional):** For added warmth or sun protection.
- **Bandana (optional):** Versatile for various uses like wiping sweat, providing sun protection for your neck, or as a makeshift dust mask.
- **Comfortable Backpack:** For carrying essentials during hikes or outings.
- **Reusable Water Bottle:** Stay hydrated throughout your trip.
- **Travel-sized toiletries:** Pack your usual toiletries or eco-friendly alternatives.

Gear:

- **Hiking Boots or Shoes:** Sturdy footwear with good traction for exploring Sedona's trails.
- **Camera:** Capture the beauty of Sedona's landscapes and experiences.
- **Phone and Charger:** Stay connected and ensure you have a portable charger for extended outings. Consider a waterproof case for added

protection.

- **Entertainment:** Download audiobooks, podcasts, or movies for long car rides or downtime at your accommodation.
- **First-Aid Kit:** Pack basic supplies like bandaids, antiseptic wipes, pain relievers, and any medications you typically use.

Medications:

- **Prescription Medications:** Bring any medications you require and pack them in your carry-on luggage.
- **Over-the-counter medications:** Consider packing pain relievers, allergy medication, or any other medications you might need.

Additional Considerations:

- **The Season:** Adapt your clothing and gear based on the time of year you're visiting. Winter requires warmer layers, while summer necessitates lighter, breathable clothing.
- **Activities:** Tailor your gear to the activities you plan. Consider bringing binoculars for birdwatching or admiring distant scenery, or trekking poles for more challenging hikes.
- **Personal Preferences:** Pack comfortable clothing that reflects your style. Consider the level of formality or informality you prefer for meals or outings.

Remember:

- Pack light and versatile clothing that can be easily mixed and matched.
- Utilize packing cubes to organize your belongings efficiently.
- Check airline baggage restrictions (weight and size allowances) to avoid excess baggage fees.

Sedona Packing List: Tailored to Your Trip Style

Here are some suggestions to tailor your Sedona packing list based on your specific travel style:

The Adventurer:

- **Hiking essentials:** Sturdy hiking boots, breathable hiking socks, moisture-wicking clothing, backpack, hiking poles (optional), and a headlamp.
- **Navigation:** Trail map, compass (learn how to use it beforehand), and a portable charger for your GPS device or phone with downloaded offline maps.
- **Sun protection:** High-SPF sunscreen, sunglasses, wide-brimmed hat, and sun gloves (optional for long hikes).
- **Hydration:** Reusable water bottle with a capacity of at least 2 liters and water purification tablets (if venturing off the beaten path).
- **Snacks:** Energy bars, trail mix, and dehydrated fruits for quick energy boosts on hikes.
- **Swimsuit:** For a refreshing dip in Oak Creek after a long hike (check regulations for designated swimming areas).

The Leisure Seeker:

- **Comfortable walking shoes:** For exploring Sedona's charming shops and streets.
- **Camera:** Capture the breathtaking scenery and unique experiences.
- **Relaxation essentials:** A good book, travel journal, swimsuit (for resorts with pools), and comfortable clothing for lounging.
- **Sunscreen and sunglasses:** Sun protection is essential year-round.
- **Reusable water bottle:** Stay hydrated throughout your sightseeing adventures.

- **Binoculars (optional):** For birdwatching or admiring distant scenery.

The Luxurious Traveler:

- **Stylish outfits:** Pack dressier options for upscale restaurants or events.
- **Comfortable walking shoes:** Balance style with comfort for exploring Sedona's townscape.
- **Camera:** Capture the beauty and luxury of your Sedona experience.
- **Sunscreen and sunglasses:** Stay protected while enjoying outdoor activities.
- **Reusable water bottle:** Eco-friendly hydration on the go.
- **Book spa treatments in advance:** Sedona offers a variety of spas. Reserve appointments beforehand to ensure availability.

Additional Considerations:

- **The Season:** Pack based on the time of year. Winter requires warmer layers, while summer necessitates lighter, breathable clothing.
- **Accommodation:** Check if your accommodation provides amenities like pool towels or robes to avoid overpacking.
- **Activities:** Tailor your clothing and gear to the activities you plan, like a hat and gloves for jeep tours in cooler weather.

Remember:

- Pack light and versatile clothing that can be easily mixed and matched.
- Utilize packing cubes to organize your belongings efficiently.
- Check airline baggage restrictions (weight and size allowances) to avoid excess baggage fees.

Essential Websites and Apps for Your Sedona Adventure

Planning & Booking:

- **Accommodation:**Visit Sedona: https://visitsedona.com/: This official Sedona tourism website offers a comprehensive listing of hotels, resorts, vacation rentals, and bed and breakfasts, allowing you to compare prices and book directly with various properties.
- Airbnb: https://www.airbnb.com/: Find unique vacation rentals and homestays, offering a taste of local living.
- https://www.booking.com/: Search for a wide range of hotels and vacation rentals with user reviews and competitive rates.
- **Flights:**Google Flights: https://www.google.com/flights: Compare flight options from different airlines and booking agents for the best fares to airports serving Sedona (Flagstaff Pulliam or Phoenix Sky Harbor).
- Skyscanner: https://www.skyscanner.com/: Another popular flight comparison tool offering deals and price alerts.
- **Car Rentals:**Kayak: Compare rental car rates from major companies operating in Sedona and nearby airports.
- https://www.rentalcars.com/: Another car rental comparison site with a user-friendly interface.

Exploring & Activities:

- **Sedona Verde Valley Chamber of Commerce:** Sedona Verde Valley Chamber of Commerce: https://sedonachamber.com/: This website provides comprehensive information on Sedona's attractions, events calendar, hiking trails, and recommended tours.
- **AllTrails:** AllTrails: https://www.alltrails.com/: Discover an extensive database of Sedona hiking trails with reviews, difficulty levels, and downloadable maps.
- **Red Rock Jeep Tours Association:** Red Rock Jeep Tours Association: Find reputable jeep tour companies offering guided adventures through

Sedona's stunning landscapes.

Navigation & Transportation:

- **Verde Shuttle:** Verde Shuttle: https://verdeshuttle.com/: Access schedules, routes, and information on Sedona's public bus system.
- **Google Maps:** A reliable navigation app for driving, walking, and cycling directions in Sedona. Download offline maps for areas with limited cell service.
- **Ride-hailing Apps:** Consider using Uber or Lyft for on-demand transportation within Sedona, especially if public transportation isn't convenient for your needs. Be prepared for potentially higher fares compared to the bus service.
- **National Weather Service:** National Weather Service: https://www.weather.gov/: Stay updated on current and forecast weather conditions for Sedona to plan your activities accordingly.
- **Dark Sky:** Dark Sky Weather: https://darksky.net/: Another weather app known for its detailed forecasts and hyperlocal weather information.

Top Attractions

Red Rock State Park

Red Rock State Park is a stunning natural jewel nestled amidst the vibrant city of Sedona, Arizona.
Here's why you should add it to your travel itinerary:

- **Breathtaking Scenery:** Red Rock boasts dramatic red sandstone formations, lush green meadows, and the vibrant waters of Oak Creek. The park offers endless opportunities for capturing breathtaking photos or simply soaking in the beauty.
- **Hiking Paradise:** Explore a network of well-maintained trails catering to all experience levels. Hike through juniper and manzanita forests, ascend for panoramic views from Chimney Rock or Coffee Pot Rock, or follow the creek for a more leisurely stroll.
- **Diverse Wildlife:** Keep your eyes peeled for a variety of birds, coyotes, javelinas, and other creatures that call Red Rock home.
- **Environmental Education:** The park's visitor center offers interactive exhibits and programs to learn about the region's geology, ecology, and cultural significance.
- **Family-Friendly Activities:** Red Rock State Park is perfect for a fun day trip with the family. Enjoy picnicking in scenic areas, rock climbing (with proper permits and guidance), or simply exploring the wonders of nature.

Location and Admission:

- Red Rock State Park is located at 1900 SR 179, Sedona, AZ 86351.
- Entrance fees are $7 for adults (14+), $4 for youth (7-13), and free for children under 6. Annual passes are also available.

How to Get There:

- **Car:** The park is easily accessible by car. From Sedona, take SR 179 south for about 2 miles. The park entrance will be on your right.
- **Public Transportation:** The Verde Shuttle offers limited service within Sedona, with a stop near the park entrance. However, relying solely on public transportation might not be ideal due to scheduling limitations. Consider ride-sharing apps like Uber or Lyft for more flexibility.

Nearest Restaurants:

- **The Coffee Pot Restaurant:** Casual American fare with a patio overlooking Chimney Rock. (Right outside the Park Entrance)
- **Hideout Grill at Bell Rock:** Southwestern cuisine with stunning views of Bell Rock. (3.7 miles from Park Entrance)
- **Cucina Rustica:** Upscale Italian cuisine in a charming setting. (4.2 miles from Park Entrance)

Nearest Attractions:

- **Bell Rock:** A towering red sandstone formation, a sacred site for the Yavapai people, and a popular spot for photography and hiking. (3.7 miles from Park Entrance)
- **Chapel of the Holy Cross:** A unique non-denominational chapel

built directly into the side of a butte, offering panoramic views of the surrounding landscape. (2.8 miles from Park Entrance)
- **Slide Rock State Park:** A short drive away, this park features natural water slides carved from the slickrock, perfect for a refreshing summer adventure. (7.8 miles from Park Entrance)

GPS Coordinates:
Red Rock State Park: 34.8214° N, 111.7833° W

Interesting Facts:

- Red Rock State Park was established in 1972 to preserve the unique geological formations and natural beauty of the area.
- The park is home to over 400 species of plants and animals.
- The red sandstone formations were created over millions of years by wind and water erosion.
- The Yavapai people consider Sedona and the surrounding areas sacred lands with significant spiritual meaning.
- Red Rock State Park has been featured in numerous movies and television shows, including "Thelma and Louise" and "An Unexpected Journey."

The Chapel of the Holy Cross

The Chapel of the Holy Cross, perched dramatically on a butte in Sedona, Arizona, is more than just a place of worship. It's a captivating landmark that blends artistic expression with spiritual reverence.

Why You Should Visit:

- **Architectural Marvel:** The chapel's unique design features a cross embedded within the red rocks, creating a breathtaking sight.

- **Spiritual Sanctuary:** Open to all faiths, the chapel offers a peaceful atmosphere for reflection and prayer.
- **Panoramic Vistas:** Enjoy stunning views of Sedona's red rock formations from the chapel's windows and surrounding grounds.
- **Artistic Inspiration:** The chapel's design is a testament to the vision of sculptor Marguerite Brunswig Staude and architect August K. Strotz.
- **Historic Significance:** Completed in 1956, the Chapel of the Holy Cross has become a beloved landmark and symbol of Sedona.

Location and Admission:

- The Chapel of the Holy Cross is situated at 780 Chapel Rd, Sedona, AZ 86336.
- **Free Entry:** There is no admission fee to enter the chapel, but donations are gratefully accepted.

How to Get There:

- **Car:** The chapel is easily accessible by car. From Sedona, take SR 179 south for approximately 4.5 miles. Turn left onto Chapel Road and follow it for about 1 mile to the chapel parking area.
- **Public Transportation:** The Verde Shuttle offers limited service within Sedona, with a stop near the midpoint of Chapel Road. However, inconvenient schedules might necessitate ride-sharing apps like Uber or Lyft for more flexibility.

Nearest Restaurants:

- **The Coffee Pot Restaurant:** Casual American fare with a patio overlooking Chimney Rock, located right outside the Park Entrance of Red Rock State Park (2.8 miles from Chapel).

- **Hideout Grill at Bell Rock:** Southwestern cuisine with stunning views of Bell Rock (4.3 miles from Chapel).
- **Cucina Rustica:** Upscale Italian cuisine in a charming setting (4.8 miles from Chapel).

Nearest Attractions:

- **Red Rock State Park:** Explore a network of scenic trails amidst breathtaking red rock formations. (2.8 miles from Chapel)
- **Bell Rock:** A towering vortex site sacred to the Yavapai people, popular for photography and hiking. (4.3 miles from Chapel)
- **Slide Rock State Park:** Natural water slides carved from the slickrock, perfect for a refreshing summer adventure. (8.5 miles from Chapel)

GPS Coordinates:

Chapel of the Holy Cross: 34.8417° N, 111.7878° W

Interesting Facts:

- The Chapel of the Holy Cross was built from 1954 to 1956 with upwards of 25 tons of rock moved without using dynamite.
- The chapel is a Roman Catholic chapel under the auspices of the Diocese of Phoenix.
- The design was inspired by a similar chapel in Norway visited by Marguerite Brunswig Staude.
- The Chapel of the Holy Cross was awarded the American Institute of Architects' Award of Honor in 1957.
- The chapel attracts over 1 million visitors annually, making it one of Sedona's most popular attractions.

Slide Rock State Park

Calling all water enthusiasts and adventure seekers! Slide Rock State Park in Sedona, Arizona, offers a unique and refreshing escape unlike any other.

Why You Should Visit:

- **Natural Water Slides:** The park's crown jewel is a series of natural slickrock formations carved by Oak Creek over millennia, creating exhilarating natural water slides. Perfect for a fun-filled day splashing and cooling off in the Arizona sun.
- **Scenic Beauty:** Nestled amidst towering red rock formations and lush vegetation, Slide Rock offers stunning scenery alongside the water fun.
- **Family-Friendly Activities:** A perfect spot for a day trip with the family. Kids and adults alike can enjoy the water slides, have picnics amidst the scenery, or explore the park's trails.
- **Hiking Opportunities:** While the water slides are the main attraction, the park also features hiking trails offering breathtaking views of Oak Creek Canyon.
- **Wildlife Spotting:** Keep your eyes peeled for diverse bird species, squirrels, and other creatures that call Slide Rock home.

Location and Admission Tickets:
- Slide Rock State Park is located at 4000 SR 89A, Sedona, AZ 86351.
- **Admission Fees:** There is a daily entrance fee. Prices vary depending on the season, with adults (14+) typically ranging from $20-$30, and reduced rates for children and seniors. Annual passes are also available.

How to Get There:
- **Car:** The park is easily accessible by car. From Sedona, take SR 179 north for approximately 5 miles, then turn west onto SR 89A for about 2.5 miles. The park entrance will be on your right.
- **Public Transportation:** The Verde Shuttle offers limited service within Sedona, with a stop some distance from the park entrance. Consider ride-sharing apps like Uber or Lyft for more flexibility.

Nearest Restaurants:
- **Slide Rock Cafe:** Convenient option located within the park offering American cuisine, snacks, and beverages.
- **The Hideaway House:** Casual American fare with a patio overlooking Chimney Rock (3.8 miles from Park Entrance).
- **Cucina Rustica:** Upscale Italian cuisine in a charming setting (6.3 miles from Park Entrance).

Nearest Attractions:
- **Bell Rock:** A towering vortex site sacred to the Yavapai people, popular for photography and hiking. (6.3 miles from Park Entrance)
- **Chapel of the Holy Cross:** A unique chapel perched on a butte offering stunning views and spiritual significance. (7.3 miles from Park Entrance)
- **Red Rock State Park:** Explore a network of trails amidst breathtaking red rock formations. (7.8 miles from Park Entrance)

GPS Coordinates:

Slide Rock State Park: 34.8783° N, 111.7333° W

Interesting Facts:

- Slide Rock State Park was established in 1987 to protect the unique natural water slides and the surrounding ecosystem.
- The red rock formations in the park are millions of years old and were created from ancient seabeds.
- The water temperature in Oak Creek typically stays cool year-round, making it perfect for a refreshing summer adventure.
- Slide Rock State Park is a popular filming location and has been featured in movies and television shows.
- Due to its popularity, the park can get crowded, especially during peak season. Consider arriving early or visiting during weekdays for a less crowded experience.

Tlaquepaque Arts & Shopping Village

Nestled amidst the vibrant red rocks of Sedona, Tlaquepaque Arts & Shopping Village offers a delightful escape for art enthusiasts, casual strollers, and anyone seeking a taste of Southwestern charm.

Why You Should Visit:

- **Art Lover's Paradise:** Explore a curated collection of galleries showcasing an array of artistic mediums like paintings, sculptures, pottery, jewelry, and more. Meet local and regional artists, and discover one-of-a-kind pieces to add a touch of Sedona to your collection.
- **Architectural Gem:** The village itself is a work of art, featuring charm-

ing adobe architecture, courtyards adorned with colorful fountains, and pathways lined with vibrant flowers.

- **Relaxing Atmosphere:** Escape the hustle and bustle and immerse yourself in the tranquil ambiance of Tlaquepaque. Wander through the galleries at your own pace, savor a coffee or meal, and soak up the artistic energy.
- **Live Entertainment:** The village frequently features live music performances, adding another layer of cultural immersion to your visit.
- **Family-Friendly Outing:** While art enthusiasts will find a treasure trove, Tlaquepaque offers something for everyone. Kids can enjoy the vibrant atmosphere, explore unique shops, or grab a sweet treat at a local bakery.

Location and Admission:

- Tlaquepaque Arts & Shopping Village is situated at 336 S Main St, Sedona, AZ 86336.
- **Free Admission:** There's no entry fee to explore the village and browse the shops. Individual shops may have varying pricing for their products.

How to Get There:

- **Car:** The village is easily accessible by car. From Uptown Sedona, head south on SR 89A for about 0.5 miles. Turn right onto Main Street, and the village will be on your left. Free parking is available on-site.
- **Public Transportation:** The Verde Shuttle runs within Sedona and has a stop near Tlaquepaque, making it a convenient option for those relying on public transportation.

Nearest Restaurants:
- **Cucina Rustica:** Upscale Italian cuisine in a charming setting, located right across the street from Tlaquepaque.
- **The Coffee Pot Restaurant:** Casual American fare with a patio overlooking Chimney Rock (short drive from Tlaquepaque).
- **Elote Cafe:** Vibrant Mexican cuisine with a focus on fresh, local ingredients (short drive from Tlaquepaque).

Nearest Attractions:
- **Bell Rock Path Trail:** Hike to the base of the iconic Bell Rock formation for stunning views and a connection to a significant vortex site (short drive from Tlaquepaque).
- **Chapel of the Holy Cross:** A unique chapel perched on a butte, offering breathtaking vistas and spiritual significance (short drive from Tlaquepaque).
- **Red Rock State Park:** Explore a network of scenic trails amidst captivating red rock formations (short drive from Tlaquepaque).

GPS Coordinates:
Tlaquepaque Arts & Shopping Village: 34.8697° N, 111.7897° W

Interesting Facts:
- Tlaquepaque (pronounced tla-keh-pah-keh) means "place of old things" in the Nahuatl language, reflecting the village's focus on Southwestern art and culture.
- The village was established in the 1970s and has become a popular tourist destination in Sedona.

- Tlaquepaque is known for its commitment to showcasing the works of local and regional artists, ensuring visitors discover unique pieces.
- The village frequently hosts special events and art exhibitions, offering even more reasons to visit.
- Tlaquepaque's architecture and setting create a picturesque atmosphere, making it a favorite spot for photographers and anyone seeking a charming Sedona experience.

Cathedral Rock

Towering over Sedona with its dramatic presence, Cathedral Rock is a natural sandstone butte and one of the most photographed landmarks in Arizona. It's a must-visit for anyone seeking stunning scenery, a challenging hike, or a connection to Sedona's spiritual vortexes.

Why You Should Visit:

- **Unforgettable Scenery:** Cathedral Rock's unique shape and vibrant red hues provide endless opportunities for capturing breathtaking photos. Hike to different vantage points for a closer look or to appreciate the vastness of the surrounding landscape.
- **Thrilling Challenge:** For the adventurous, Cathedral Rock offers a challenging but rewarding hike. The trail leads you up steep inclines, requiring scrambling and navigating uneven terrain. The sense of accomplishment at the summit, along with the panoramic views, makes it worthwhile for experienced hikers.
- **Spiritual Significance:** Cathedral Rock is considered a powerful vortex site by some, believed to be a center of energy and spiritual awakening. Whether you're a believer or not, the atmosphere invites reflection and appreciation for the beauty of nature.
- **Wildlife Spotting:** Keep your eyes peeled for hawks soaring overhead,

lizards basking on the rocks, or rabbits darting through the vegetation.

- **Family-Friendly Option:** Even if you don't attempt the summit hike, the Cathedral Rock Trail offers a moderate climb with scenic views, suitable for families with older children.

Location and Admission:

- Cathedral Rock is situated near the center of Sedona, just off Back O' Beyond Road.
- There is no entrance fee to access the Cathedral Rock Trail itself. However, parking can be a challenge, especially during peak season. The Red Rock Pass system applies to nearby parking areas, with fees ranging from $5-$10 per day.

How to Get There:

- **Car:** The trailhead is easily accessible by car. From Uptown Sedona, take SR 179 south for approximately 1.5 miles. Turn right onto Back O' Beyond Road and follow it for about 0.6 miles. The trailhead parking lot will be on your left.
- **Public Transportation:** The Verde Shuttle offers limited service within Sedona, with a stop somewhat distant from the trailhead. Consider ride-sharing services like Uber or Lyft for more flexibility, especially if parking availability is a concern.

Nearest Restaurants:

- **The Coffee Pot Restaurant:** Casual American fare with a patio overlooking Chimney Rock (right outside the Park Entrance of Red Rock State Park). (Short drive from Cathedral Rock)

- **Hideout Grill at Bell Rock:** Southwestern cuisine with stunning views of Bell Rock (3.7 miles from Cathedral Rock Trailhead).
- **Cucina Rustica:** Upscale Italian cuisine in a charming setting (4.2 miles from Cathedral Rock Trailhead).

Nearest Attractions:

- **Red Rock State Park:** Explore a network of scenic trails amidst breathtaking red rock formations. (Adjacent to Cathedral Rock)
- **Bell Rock Path Trail:** Hike to the base of the iconic Bell Rock formation for stunning views and a connection to a significant vortex site (3.7 miles from Cathedral Rock Trailhead).
- **Chapel of the Holy Cross:** A unique chapel perched on a butte, offering breathtaking vistas and spiritual significance (2.8 miles from Cathedral Rock Trailhead).

GPS Coordinates:
Cathedral Rock Trailhead: 34.8191° N, 111.7932° W

Interesting Facts:

- Cathedral Rock was once called "Court House Rock" on some early maps, and Courthouse Butte was called "Church House Rock," which has caused confusion ever since.
- The iconic saddle formation at the top of Cathedral Rock is known as "The Knees."
- Cathedral Rock has been featured in numerous movies and television shows, including "Westworld," "Thelma and Louise," and "An American Tail: Fievel Goes West."
- Climbers from around the world visit Sedona to attempt the challenging ascent of Cathedral Rock. However, proper permits and technical

expertise are mandatory due to safety risks.

- Respect the sanctity of Cathedral Rock for those who consider it a spiritual site. Be mindful of noise levels and maintain a clean environment by packing out all trash.

Devil's Bridge

Devil's Bridge, a natural sandstone arch perched precariously over a deep chasm, is an iconic landmark in Sedona, Arizona. It beckons adventurous souls and curious minds with its unique formation and intriguing local legends.

Why You Should Visit:

- **Geological Marvel:** Witness the power of nature as you stand beneath this massive arch, sculpted by millions of years of erosion. Devil's Bridge offers a captivating example of Sedona's remarkable geologic formations.
- **Thrilling Hike:** The hike to Devil's Bridge is moderate with some steeper sections and uneven terrain. The reward is not only reaching the bridge but also experiencing stunning views of the surrounding landscape.
- **Local Legends:** The bridge's name is steeped in folklore. Some stories say it was built by the devil himself, while others claim it holds special spiritual significance.
- **Photographic Opportunity:** Capture the impressive scale of Devil's Bridge and the dramatic Sedona scenery as a backdrop.
- **Adventure for All:** While the bridge itself is not accessible for walking across due to safety concerns, the hike offers a fun adventure for those in decent physical condition.

Location and Admission Fee

27

- Devil's Bridge is located within the Devil's Bridge Trail System in West Sedona.
- There is no entrance fee to access the trailhead. However, parking can be limited, especially during peak season. The Red Rock Pass system applies to nearby parking areas, with fees ranging from $5-$10 per day.

How to Get There:

- **Car:** The trailhead is accessible by car. From Uptown Sedona, take SR 179 north for approximately 4.5 miles. Turn left onto Dry Creek Road and follow it for about 1.5 miles. Turn right onto Long Canyon Road and continue for 0.3 miles. The trailhead parking lot will be on your right.
- **Public Transportation:** Verde Shuttle service within Sedona is limited and doesn't reach the Devil's Bridge Trailhead directly. Consider ride-sharing apps like Uber or Lyft for more flexibility, especially if parking availability is a concern.

Nearest Restaurants:

- **Hideout Grill at Bell Rock:** Southwestern cuisine with stunning views of Bell Rock (3.7 miles from the Dry Creek Vista Trailhead).
- **The Creekside Restaurant at Oak Creek Canyon:** Casual American fare with a patio overlooking Oak Creek (4.8 miles from the Dry Creek Vista Trailhead).
- **Cucina Rustica:** Upscale Italian cuisine in a charming setting (6.3 miles from the Dry Creek Vista Trailhead).

Nearest Attractions:

- **Bell Rock Path Trail:** Hike to the base of the iconic Bell Rock formation for stunning views and a connection to a significant vortex site (4.3 miles from the Dry Creek Vista Trailhead).

- **Slide Rock State Park:** Natural water slides carved from the slickrock, perfect for a refreshing summer adventure (7.8 miles from the Dry Creek Vista Trailhead) .
- **Chapel of the Holy Cross:** A unique chapel perched on a butte, offering breathtaking vistas and spiritual significance (7.3 miles from the Dry Creek Vista Trailhead).

GPS Coordinates:

Dry Creek Vista Trailhead (leading to Devil's Bridge): 34.8903° N, 111.7701° W

Interesting Facts:

- The name "Devil's Bridge" has likely been around for generations, with various stories and legends emerging to explain its unique formation.
- Devil's Bridge is not a natural arch in the strictest sense, but rather a freestanding fin of rock. Over time, erosion may cause it to collapse, so appreciate its presence in its current form.
- The hike to Devil's Bridge can get busy, especially during peak season. Arrive early or plan your visit for weekdays to avoid large crowds.
- Respect the fragile environment. Stay on designated trails and avoid climbing on the bridge itself for safety reasons.

Grand Canyon Journeys

Grand Canyon Journeys is the official concessionaire of the National Park Service for the South Rim of the Grand Canyon. They offer a variety of tours and packages that allow visitors to experience the Grand Canyon in a unique and unforgettable way.

Reason to Visit

- **Expert Guides:** Their tours are led by knowledgeable and experienced guides who can share interesting facts and stories about the canyon's geology, history, and culture.
- **Variety of Tours:** They offer a variety of tours to suit different interests and abilities, from narrated bus tours to more adventurous hikes and rafting trips.
- **Unique Access:** Some of their tours offer access to areas of the canyon that are not accessible to the general public, such as the rim-to-rim railroad tour.
- **Hassle-Free Experience:** They take care of all the logistics, so you can relax and enjoy your Grand Canyon experience.

Location

Grand Canyon National Park is located in northwestern Arizona, USA. The South Rim is the most popular and easily accessible section of the canyon. Grand Canyon Journeys operates out of the South Rim Grand Canyon Village.

Admission Tickets

Entrance fees to Grand Canyon National Park are required for all visitors. Tour prices vary depending on the specific tour you choose. Here are the current entrance fees:

- Adults (16 years and older): $35 (valid for 7 days)
- Children (6-15 years old): $15 (valid for 7 days)
- Individuals 62 and older: $30 (valid for lifetime)

How to Get There

The South Rim of the Grand Canyon can be reached by car, bus, or airplane. The nearest major airport is McCarran International Airport in Las Vegas, Nevada, approximately 270 miles from the South Rim.

Here are the addresses for the South Rim Visitor Center and the Grand Canyon Railway Depot:

- **South Rim Visitor Center**Address: South Entrance Station, Grand Canyon National Park, AZ 86023
- GPS Coordinates: 35.9994° N, -112.1141° W
- **Grand Canyon Railway Depot**Address: 233 E. Butler Ave., Williams, AZ 86046
- GPS Coordinates: 35.2397° N, -112.190° W

Nearest Restaurants

There are a variety of restaurants located within Grand Canyon National Park at the South Rim. Here are a few options:

- **El Tovar Dining Room:** This fine-dining restaurant offers stunning views of the canyon and a menu of Southwestern cuisine.
- **Maswik Food Court:** This casual food court offers a variety of quick and affordable options, including pizza, burgers, and sandwiches.
- **Black Canyon Coffee Shop:** This coffee shop offers a variety of coffees, teas, and pastries.

Nearest Attractions

In addition to the Grand Canyon itself, there are a number of other attractions located near the South Rim. Here are a few suggestions:

- **Grand Canyon Village:** This historic village is home to a variety of shops, restaurants, and lodging options.

- **Yavapai Geology Museum:** This museum offers exhibits on the geology, history, and ecology of the Grand Canyon.
- **Mather Point:** This is one of the most popular viewpoints on the South Rim, offering stunning views of the canyon.

Interesting Facts

- The Grand Canyon is one of the Seven Natural Wonders of the World.
- The canyon is 277 miles (446 km) long, up to 18 miles (29 km) wide and attains a depth of over a mile (6,093 feet or 1,857 meters).
- The canyon was formed by the Colorado River over millions of years.
- The canyon is home to a variety of plant and animal life, including many species that are found nowhere else on earth.

Transportation

While Sedona itself doesn't have a commercial airport that handles regular flights, there are a few conveniently located airports that serve the area, each with its own advantages:

1. Flagstaff Pulliam Airport (FLG)

- Distance from Sedona: 23 miles (40-minute drive)
- Location: Flagstaff, Arizona (just south of downtown)
- Services: This is the closest commercial airport to Sedona with several airlines including United and American Airlines offering connecting flights through Phoenix Sky Harbor Airport (PHX) and other major hubs. Limited car rental options are available, shuttle services, and taxi services are available for hire.
- Contact: (928) 774-6623

Transportation Options:

- Car Rentals: Major car rental companies are available at the airport.
- Shuttles: Several shuttle companies offer rides to Sedona from the airport, costing around $40-$60 per person. These can be booked in advance or upon arrival.
- Taxis: Taxis are available at the airport, but be prepared for a higher fare (around $80-$100) to Sedona.
- Special Deals/Discounts: Airlines frequently offer special deals and

discounts, particularly during the off-season (winter). It's recommended to check the websites of desired airlines and subscribe to their email alerts for updates on special offers.

Tips for Navigating the Airport:
Flagstaff Pulliam Airport is a relatively small airport, so it's easy to navigate. Security lines are usually short, but allow ample time to check in for your flight, especially during peak season.

2. Phoenix Sky Harbor International Airport (PHX)

- Distance from Sedona: 119 miles (2-hour drive)
- Location: Phoenix, Arizona
- Services: This is a major international airport with numerous airlines offering both domestic and international flights. A wide variety of services are available including car rentals, shuttles, taxis, and rideshare options like Uber and Lyft.
- Contact: (602) 244-2400

Transportation Options:

- Car Rentals: All major car rental companies are represented at the Phoenix Sky Harbor International Airport.
- Shuttles: Several shuttle companies offer shared-ride or private van services to Sedona, costing around $80-$120 per person.
- Taxis: Taxis are readily available, but be prepared for a hefty fare (around $200-$250) to Sedona.
- Ridesharing: Ridesharing services like Uber and Lyft are available at the airport and can be a more affordable option compared to taxis, especially for multiple passengers.
- Special Deals/Discounts: Similar to Flagstaff Pulliam Airport, airlines serving Phoenix Sky Harbor International Airport frequently offer special deals and discounts. It's recommended to check the websites

of the airlines you're considering and sign up for email alerts to receive updates on special offers.

Tips for Navigating the Airport:

- Phoenix Sky Harbor International Airport is a large and busy airport. Familiarize yourself with the airport layout before you travel and allow plenty of time for checking in, security lines, and potential delays. Download the Phoenix Sky Harbor app to your smartphone for real-time flight information, terminal maps, and concessionaire listings.

3. Sedona Airport (SEZ)

- Distance from Sedona: 2 miles (15-minute drive)
- Location: Just southwest of Sedona's town center
- Services: This is a general aviation airport that does not offer scheduled commercial flights. It primarily caters to private planes, air tours, and sightseeing adventures.
- Contact: (928) 282-5991

Transportation Options:

- Taxis: Taxis may be available upon request, but having a pre-arranged car service is recommended as taxis are not always readily available at the airport.
- Ridesharing: Ridesharing services like Uber and Lyft are not available at the airport and may be difficult to hail in the immediate area.

Choosing the Right Airport:
The best airport for you depends on your priorities. Here's a quick guide:

- **Convenience:** Flagstaff Pulliam Airport is the closest with the shortest travel time to

Flagstaff Pulliam Airport (FLG):

- **Pros:** Closest airport to Sedona (40-minute drive), offers connecting flights on major airlines, potentially shorter security lines.
- **Cons:** Limited car rental options, fewer flight options compared to PHX, shuttle services can be more expensive.

Phoenix Sky Harbor International Airport (PHX):

- **Pros:** Major international airport with the most flight options and potentially lower fares, wider variety of transportation choices (including rideshare), more car rental options.
- **Cons:** Furthest distance from Sedona (2-hour drive), potentially longer security lines due to larger airport size, more expensive transportation options (especially taxis) to Sedona.

Sedona Airport (SEZ):

- **Pros:** Closest to Sedona (15-minute drive), potentially interesting for scenic flights or air tours.
- **Cons:** No scheduled commercial flights, requires arranging private transportation to/from the airport.

Here's a recommendation based on travel style:

- **Budget Traveler:** Consider Flagstaff Pulliam Airport with its shorter travel time and potentially lower shuttle fares. Look for deals on connecting flights through major hubs.
- **Time-Conscious Traveler:** If minimizing travel time is your priority, Flagstaff Pulliam Airport is the best option.
- **Convenience Seeker:** Phoenix Sky Harbor International Airport offers the most flight options and a wider variety of transportation choices,

although it comes with a longer travel time to Sedona. Consider ridesharing for a more affordable option compared to taxis.

- **Luxury Traveler:** Flying into Phoenix Sky Harbor and arranging a private car service to Sedona might be the most convenient option. Additionally, Sedona Airport could be an option if you're interested in a scenic flight or air tour upon arrival.

Additional Tips:

- **Compare flight prices:** Look at airfare on different airlines and booking sites to find the best deal. Consider the total cost, including baggage fees and potential transportation costs from the airport to Sedona.
- **Factor in travel time:** While Flagstaff Pulliam Airport is closer, consider the time it takes to get a connecting flight there compared to a potentially non-stop flight into Phoenix.
- **Plan your transportation:** If you're not renting a car, research shuttle services, rideshare availability, or pre-arrange a car service before your trip.

Car Rentals and Driving Essentials

While Sedona offers a charming atmosphere, exploring its surrounding beauty often requires a car.

Car Rental Services:

- **Major Companies:** Several reputable car rental companies operate in Sedona, including Enterprise, Avis, Budget, and Eagle Rent a Car. These companies typically have offices located either within Sedona or at the nearby Flagstaff Pulliam Airport.
- **Special Deals and Discounts:** Car rental companies frequently offer

deals and discounts, particularly during the off-season (winter). Check their websites and subscribe to email alerts for updates. Consider joining the loyalty program of your preferred company to unlock potential benefits.

Tips for Choosing a Car:

- **Sedan:** Suitable for most paved roads within Sedona, offering good gas mileage.
- **SUV:** Ideal for venturing off-road on designated trails and providing extra space for luggage or gear.
- **Jeep Wrangler:** Popular choice for off-road enthusiasts, offering an open-air experience (consider weather conditions).
- **Fuel Efficiency:** Gas prices can fluctuate, so consider a fuel-efficient option, especially if planning extensive driving.

Driving Regulations:

- **General Rules:** US traffic laws apply, with right-of-way at intersections following standard protocols.
- **Speed Limits:** Be aware of posted speed limits, which can vary significantly between highways, scenic routes, and in-town areas.
- **Seatbelts:** Seatbelt usage is mandatory for all occupants.
- **Cell Phone Use:** Hands-free devices are required while driving.
- **Parking:** Pay attention to parking signs and restrictions, especially in popular tourist areas.

Navigating the Roadways:

- **Maps and GPS:** While GPS navigation is helpful, having a physical map as a backup is advisable, especially in areas with limited cell service.
- **Scenic Routes:** Sedona offers stunning scenery. Consider scenic drives

like the Red Rock Scenic Byway or explore the switchbacks of Oak Creek Canyon, all while adhering to posted speed limits.

- **Wildlife:** Be cautious of wildlife, particularly deer, which can dart across the road unexpectedly.
- **Off-Roading:** Only use designated off-road trails to avoid damaging the fragile ecosystem.

Making the Most of Your Driving Experience:

- **Download Offline Maps:** Download offline maps on your phone's navigation app to avoid relying solely on cellular data.
- **Pack Essentials:** Keep a water bottle, snacks, and sunscreen readily available, especially on longer drives.
- **Enjoy the Scenery:** Pull over at designated viewpoints to soak in the breathtaking views and capture those perfect Sedona moments.
- **Be Prepared:** Check the weather forecast before heading out. Consider carrying basic emergency supplies like a flashlight, jumper cables, and a first-aid kit.

Additional Tips:

- **Book Your Car in Advance:** Especially during peak seasons, rentals can get booked quickly. Reserve your car well in advance to avoid last-minute hassles.
- **Review Insurance Coverage:** Understand your car rental insurance coverage and consider purchasing additional coverage if needed.
- **Fuel Up Before Returning:** Most rental companies charge a fee if the car is not returned with a full tank of gas.

Public Transportation Options

While Sedona isn't known for its extensive public transportation network, there are some options available for budget-conscious travelers or those wanting to minimize their environmental impact.

Bus Services:

- **Verde Shuttle:** This public transit route connects central Cottonwood with West Sedona, Uptown Sedona, and northern portions of State Route 179 (SR 179). It operates seven days a week with multiple trips throughout the day [Verde Shuttle: https://verdeshuttle.com/].
- **Routes:** The Verde Shuttle operates along a designated route with stops throughout Sedona and Cottonwood. Schedules and maps are available on their website.
- **Schedules:** Schedules vary depending on the day of the week. Check the Verde Shuttle website for the most current schedule information.
- **Pricing:** Fares are affordable, typically around $2-$4 per ride with potential discounts for seniors and students (exact fares are subject to change, so verify on the Verde Shuttle website).
- **Tips:** Purchase tickets onboard or consider purchasing a day pass for unlimited rides if you plan on using the service extensively.

Absence of Subway and Train Services:

- Sedona does not have a subway or train system. These modes of public transportation are typically found in larger metropolitan areas.

Making the Most of Public Transportation:

- **Plan Your Trip:** Public transportation can take longer than driving. Plan your itinerary carefully, considering bus schedules and potential wait times.

- **Download Apps:** Download the Verde Shuttle app (if available) for real-time tracking and schedule updates.
- **Purchase Tickets in Advance:** Consider purchasing day passes or pre-loading a travel card (if offered) to save time and avoid fumbling with cash onboard.
- **Carry Essentials:** Pack water, snacks, and entertainment for potential waits between bus connections.
- **Enjoy the Ride:** Public transportation allows you to relax and enjoy the scenery without the stress of driving and parking.

Additional Considerations:

- **Limited Service:** Public transportation options in Sedona are limited compared to larger cities. They may not reach all destinations you desire to visit.
- **Accessibility:** While the Verde Shuttle is accessible with designated areas for wheelchairs and scooters, verify accessibility features if you have specific needs.
- **Taxis and Ridesharing:** Taxis and ridesharing services like Uber and Lyft are available in Sedona, but fares can be higher compared to the bus service. Consider these options for on-demand transportation or reaching areas not serviced by the Verde Shuttle.

Accommodation

A Sunset Chateau

A Sunset Chateau is a boutique bed and breakfast nestled amidst the breathtaking red rock formations of Sedona, Arizona. This luxurious escape offers panoramic views, artistically decorated suites, and personalized service, making it the perfect haven for a romantic getaway or a rejuvenating retreat.

About :

A Sunset Chateau is a family-owned and operated property with a focus on warmth, hospitality, and creating unforgettable guest experiences. The property boasts stunning views of Sedona's iconic red rocks and offers a peaceful ambiance surrounded by nature.

Property Amenities:

- **Outdoor Pool and Jacuzzi:** Take a refreshing dip in the saltwater pool or unwind in the jacuzzi while soaking in the captivating red rock views. A kiva fireplace adds a touch of ambiance during evenings.
- **Lush Gardens and Patios:** Relax amidst meticulously landscaped gardens, offering a tranquil escape and plenty of space to unwind. Patio seating allows you to enjoy the fresh air and breathtaking scenery.
- **Free Wi-Fi:** Stay connected with complimentary high-speed Wi-Fi throughout the property.

- **Free Parking:** On-site parking is available for guests.

Room Features:

- **Luxurious Suites:** Choose from a variety of casita suites, each offering ample space, comfortable furnishings, and unique curated artwork.
- **Fireplaces and Kitchens:** Many suites feature cozy electric fireplaces, perfect for creating a warm and inviting atmosphere. Some suites also include fully equipped kitchenettes for added convenience.
- **Private Patios or Balconies:** Enjoy your morning coffee or an evening glass of wine on your private patio or balcony, taking in the mesmerizing red rock vistas.
- **Modern Amenities:** All suites come equipped with modern conveniences like flat-screen TVs with cable access and organic bath amenities.

Average Cost:

The average cost per night at A Sunset Chateau can range from $329 to upwards of $500 per night.

Nearest Attractions:

- **Hiking Trails:** Several hiking trails are located right across the street from the property, offering easy access to exploring Sedona's stunning red rock formations. Popular options include Airport Mesa Loop Trail and Bell Rock Path.
- **Chapel of the Holy Cross:** This iconic landmark, a small chapel built into the side of a butte, is a short drive away and offers scenic views.
- **Art Galleries and Shops:** Sedona is renowned for its vibrant art scene. Explore the many art galleries and shops in town showcasing local artists and handcrafted souvenirs.

Nearest Restaurant:

- **Twisted Vine Sedona:** Located within walking distance of the hotel, Twisted Vine offers upscale American cuisine with a focus on fresh, seasonal ingredients and stunning red rock views.

Links and Contact:

- Website: https://asunsetchateau.com/contact-us/
- Contact: (928) 963-1782

Adobe Grand Villas

Nestled amidst the awe-inspiring red rocks of Sedona, Arizona, Adobe Grand Villas offers a luxurious and intimate bed and breakfast experience. This upscale boutique property caters to discerning travelers seeking a haven of relaxation, gourmet dining, and personalized service.

About the Accommodation :

Adobe Grand Villas exudes a refined charm, blending traditional Southwestern architecture with modern amenities. Personalized attention and a focus on guest comfort create an unforgettable stay in the heart of Sedona's magic.

Property Amenities:

- **Year-round Heated Pool and Spa:** Unwind in the sparkling outdoor pool or soothe your muscles in the jacuzzi, all surrounded by the beauty of the red rock landscape.
- **Beautiful Lush Landscaping:** Stroll through meticulously maintained gardens offering a tranquil escape and a connection with nature.

- **Fully-Stocked Coffee and Tea Bar:** Start your day with a cup of freshly brewed coffee or unwind in the afternoon with a selection of fine teas.
- **Fresh Homemade Cookies:** A touch of hospitality awaits you with complimentary homemade cookies served throughout the day.
- **Complimentary Concierge Services:** The knowledgeable concierge team is happy to assist you with activity planning, restaurant reservations, and recommendations to enhance your Sedona experience.
- **Wireless Internet Access:** Stay connected with complimentary Wi-Fi throughout the property.
- **Free Parking:** On-site parking is available for guests.

Room Features:

- **Exquisitely Designed Villas:** Choose from a variety of spacious villas, each boasting custom design, handcrafted details, and a private entrance.
- **Fireplaces and Private Patios/Balconies:** Cozy up by a crackling fireplace (in most rooms) or relax on your private patio or balcony, taking in the breathtaking red rock views.
- **Jetted Two-Person Tubs:** Indulge in a relaxing soak in the luxurious jetted tub, perfect for unwinding after a day of exploration.
- **Kitchenettes with Microwaves and Refrigerators:** In-room kitchenettes provide added convenience for preparing light meals or snacks.
- **Luxury Linens and Bathrobes:** Wrap yourself in comfort with plush linens and luxurious bathrobes provided for your stay.
- **Premium Entertainment:** Enjoy a movie night or catch up on your favorite shows with a flat-screen TV and DirecTV access.

Average Cost:

The average cost per night at Adobe Grand Villas varies from $450 to upwards of $800 per night.

Nearest Attractions:

- **Hiking Trails:** Sedona offers a plethora of hiking trails to suit all levels. Popular choices include West Fork Trail and Chimney Rock Trail, both located within a short drive of the property.
- **Tlaquepaque Arts and Crafts Village:** Explore this charming art village showcasing a variety of galleries, shops, and restaurants, all nestled amidst a vibrant cultural atmosphere.
- **Jeep Tours:** Embark on an adventurous jeep tour through Sedona's rugged terrain and discover hidden canyons and mesmerizing rock formations.

Nearest Restaurant:

- **Elote Cafe:** Located a short distance away, Elote Cafe offers a delectable Southwestern cuisine experience with a focus on fresh, local ingredients.

Hotel Links and Contact:

- Website: https://www.adobegrandvillas.com/
- Contact: (800) 249-3797

Location:

Adobe Grand Villas is situated at 350 Laughlin Lane, Sedona, Arizona 86351, USA.

Languages Spoken:

The staff at Adobe Grand Villas is likely to speak English fluently. For information on other languages spoken by the staff, it's recommended to contact the property directly

The Inn Above Oak Creek

The Inn Above Oak Creek, nestled amidst the breathtaking red rocks and towering pines of Sedona, Arizona, offers a tranquil escape for discerning travelers. This charming inn provides a unique blend of rustic elegance, personalized service, and stunning natural beauty, making it the perfect retreat for a romantic getaway or a rejuvenating vacation.

About the Inn:
The Inn Above Oak Creek boasts a rich history dating back to the 1930s. The original lodge, built with native stone and timbers, exudes a timeless charm. The inn prioritizes guest comfort and tranquility, offering a peaceful haven surrounded by the wonders of Sedona.

Property Amenities:

- **Heated Pool and Jacuzzi:** Unwind after a day of exploration in the sparkling, seasonally heated pool or soothe your muscles in the jacuzzi, all while surrounded by the captivating scenery.
- **Picturesque Gardens and Patios:** Stroll through meticulously landscaped gardens bursting with colorful flora, offering a peaceful escape and a connection with nature. Relax on the patios and soak in the breathtaking views of Oak Creek Canyon and the red rock formations.
- **Complimentary Breakfast:** Fuel your day with a delicious complimentary breakfast served each morning, featuring a variety of seasonal dishes and local ingredients.
- **BBQ Grills:** Enjoy an intimate cookout under the stars with access to on-site barbecue grills.
- **Wireless Internet Access:** Stay connected with complimentary Wi-Fi throughout the property.
- **Free Parking:** On-site parking is available for guests.

Room Features:

- **Unique Accommodations:** Choose from a variety of rooms and suites, each offering a distinctive character and a blend of rustic charm with modern amenities.
- **Fireplaces and Balconies:** Cozy up by a crackling fireplace (available in most rooms) or relax on your private balcony, taking in the breathtaking views of Oak Creek Canyon or the red rock formations.
- **Jetted Tubs:** Indulge in a relaxing soak in the jetted tub featured in many rooms, perfect for unwinding after a day of adventure.
- **Luxury Linens and Bath Amenities:** Wrap yourself in comfort with plush linens and luxurious bath amenities provided for your stay.
- **In-Room Coffee Maker and Refrigerator:** Enjoy the convenience of an in-room coffee maker and refrigerator for preparing light meals or snacks.

Average Cost:

The average cost per night at The Inn Above Oak Creek varies depending on the season, room type, and occupancy. Generally, rates range from $250 to upwards of $500 per night.

Nearest Attraction:

- **Oak Creek Canyon:** The majestic Oak Creek Canyon, right at the doorstep of the inn, offers breathtaking scenery, hiking trails, and swimming holes. Explore the natural wonders and immerse yourself in the beauty of the canyon.

Nearest Restaurant:

- **Creekside Restaurant at The Inn Above Oak Creek:** For a convenient dining option, the on-site Creekside Restaurant offers delicious meals prepared with fresh, seasonal ingredients. Enjoy stunning views of Oak Creek Canyon while savoring your meal.

Hotel Links and Contact:

- Website: https://www.innaboveoakcreek.com/
- Contact: (800) 662-9109

Location:

The Inn Above Oak Creek is situated at 3500 West State Route 89A, Sedona, Arizona 86351, USA.

Lantern Light Inn

Nestled amidst the towering red rocks of Sedona, Arizona, Lantern Light Inn offers a charming and intimate escape for travelers seeking a blend of comfort, affordability, and a touch of history. This family-run inn provides a welcoming atmosphere and a convenient location to explore the wonders of Sedona.

About the Inn:

Established in 1962, Lantern Light Inn maintains a traditional Southwestern aesthetic with a focus on warmth and hospitality. The friendly staff and cozy ambiance create a comfortable haven for your Sedona adventure.

Property Amenities:

- **Heated Pool and Jacuzzi:** Relax after a day of exploration in the sparkling, seasonally heated pool or unwind in the jacuzzi, surrounded by the beauty of Sedona's red rock landscape.

- **Landscaped Grounds with Patios:** Stroll through the well-maintained grounds featuring native plants and colorful flowers. Relax on the patios and soak in the sunshine or enjoy a cup of coffee amidst the fresh air.
- **Complimentary Continental Breakfast:** Start your day with a complimentary continental breakfast offering a selection of pastries, cereals, fruits, and beverages.
- **Barbecue Grills and Picnic Area:** Enjoy an outdoor meal with access to on-site barbecue grills and picnic tables. Perfect for a casual gathering or a cookout under the stars.
- **Wireless Internet Access:** Stay connected with complimentary Wi-Fi throughout the property.
- **Free Parking:** On-site parking is available for guests.

Room Features:

- **Comfortable Accommodations:** Choose from a variety of rooms, all offering a cozy and comfortable atmosphere.
- **Private Balconies or Patios:** Many rooms feature private balconies or patios, allowing you to relax and enjoy the fresh air or take in the views of the surrounding landscape.
- **Refrigerators and Microwaves:** In-room amenities like refrigerators and microwaves provide added convenience for storing drinks and snacks or preparing light meals.
- **Coffee Makers:** Start your day with a cup of coffee brewed in the convenience of your room.
- **Traditional Furnishings:** The rooms feature a traditional Southwestern style with comfortable furnishings and warm color palettes.

Average Cost:

The average cost per night at Lantern Light Inn varies depending on the season, room type, and occupancy. Generally, rates are more affordable compared to other Sedona properties, ranging from $150 to $300 per night.

Nearest Attraction:

- **Bell Rock:** This iconic red rock formation, a short drive from the hotel, offers scenic views and hiking trails suitable for all skill levels. Be sure to capture stunning photographs of this natural landmark.

Nearest Restaurant:

- **The Hideaway House:** Located within walking distance, The Hideaway House offers a casual dining experience with a focus on American comfort food and local ingredients.

Inn Links and Contact:

- Website: https://www.lanternlightinn.com/
- Contact: (928) 282-3371

Location:

Lantern Light Inn is situated at 505 West State Route 89A, Sedona, Arizona 86351, USA.

El Portal Sedona Hotel

El Portal Sedona Hotel, amidst the captivating red rocks of Sedona, Arizona, promises an unforgettable stay in a luxurious and stylish environment. This AAA Four-Diamond resort caters to discerning travelers seeking comfort, exceptional service, and breathtaking surroundings.

About the Hotel:

El Portal Sedona Hotel embodies elegance and sophistication, blending seamlessly with the natural beauty of Sedona. Spacious accommodations, personalized attention to detail, and a plethora of amenities guarantee a truly relaxing and rejuvenating experience.

Property Amenities:

- **Heated Swimming Pool and Infinity Hot Tub:** Unwind and soak in the breathtaking red rock views while taking a dip in the sparkling pool or relaxing in the infinity hot tub.
- **Spa Cenota:** Indulge in a variety of rejuvenating spa treatments at Spa Cenota, featuring massages, facials, and other wellness services designed to pamper your body and mind.
- **Award-Winning Restaurants:** Embark on a culinary journey at one of the hotel's two award-winning restaurants, featuring innovative dishes prepared with fresh, local ingredients.
- **State-of-the-Art Fitness Center:** Maintain your fitness routine with access to the well-equipped fitness center featuring modern exercise equipment.
- **Concierge Services:** The knowledgeable concierge team is happy to assist you with activity planning, restaurant recommendations, and making your Sedona experience unforgettable.
- **Wireless Internet Access:** Stay connected with complimentary Wi-Fi throughout the property.
- **Valet and Self-Parking Options:** Choose between convenient valet

parking or self-parking options for your vehicle.

Room Features:

- **Spacious Casitas and Suites:** Unwind in luxurious casitas or suites, each offering ample space, plush furnishings, and private balconies or patios.
- **Fireplaces and Breathtaking Views:** Cozy up by a crackling fireplace (available in most rooms) and take in the mesmerizing red rock vistas from your private balcony or patio.
- **Oversized Bathrooms:** Relax in the spa-inspired bathrooms featuring soaking tubs, separate showers, and luxurious bath amenities.
- **High-Tech Amenities:** Modern conveniences include flat-screen TVs, premium cable channels, and iHome docking stations for your devices.
- **Private Balconies or Patios:** Enjoy your morning coffee or an evening glass of wine while breathing in the fresh air and marveling at the red rock scenery.

Average Cost:

The average cost per night at El Portal Sedona Hotel varies depending on the season, room type, and occupancy. Generally, rates range from $400 to upwards of $1,000 per night.

Nearest Attraction:

- **Chimney Rock:** This iconic red rock formation, towering right behind the hotel, offers scenic views and hiking trails. Explore the natural beauty and capture stunning photographs.
- **Slide Rock State Park:** Cool off and have some fun at Slide Rock State Park, featuring natural water slides carved into the red rocks. Perfect for a refreshing afternoon adventure.

Nearest Restaurant:

- **El Portal Restaurant:** For a convenient and delectable dining experience, El Portal Restaurant on-site offers innovative Southwestern cuisine prepared with fresh, seasonal ingredients.

Hotel Links and Contact:

- Website: https://elportalsedona.com/
- Contact: (928) 282-3300

Location:

El Portal Sedona Hotel is situated at 100 Eckert Road, Sedona, Arizona 86351, USA.

Best Western Plus Arroyo Roble Hotel & Creekside Villas

Best Western Plus Arroyo Roble Hotel & Creekside Villas offers a welcoming and convenient haven for travelers seeking a comfortable and affordable stay. This family-friendly hotel boasts spacious accommodations, a variety of amenities, and easy access to Sedona's many attractions.

About the Hotel:

Best Western Plus Arroyo Roble Hotel & Creekside Villas caters to a diverse range of travelers. Choose from standard hotel rooms or opt for the privacy and space of creekside villas, perfect for families or groups. The friendly staff and relaxed atmosphere ensure a comfortable and enjoyable stay.

Property Amenities:

- **Two Outdoor Pools and Hot Tubs:** Make a splash and unwind in one of the two sparkling outdoor pools, or soothe your muscles in the relaxing hot tubs. Perfect for cooling off after a day of exploring Sedona's wonders.

- **Game Room and Playground:** Keep the kids entertained with the on-site game room featuring fun activities. A dedicated playground allows them to burn off energy while enjoying the fresh air.
- **Complimentary Breakfast:** Fuel your day with a complimentary hot breakfast buffet, offering a delicious selection of items to start your Sedona adventure.
- **Private Creek Access:** Enjoy a unique perk – direct access to Oak Creek, a refreshing escape from the Arizona sunshine. Relax by the water or explore the natural beauty of the creek.
- **Tennis and Basketball Courts:** Challenge your friends or family to a game on the on-site tennis or basketball courts.
- **Fitness Center:** Maintain your workout routine with access to the fitness center featuring exercise equipment.
- **Guest Laundry Facilities:** Take care of laundry needs with convenient on-site guest laundry facilities.
- **Wireless Internet Access:** Stay connected with complimentary Wi-Fi throughout the property.
- **Free Parking:** Ample on-site parking is available for guests.

Room Features:

- **Comfortable Accommodations:** Choose from standard hotel rooms or spacious creekside villas, all offering comfortable furnishings and a relaxed atmosphere.
- **Red Rock Views:** Many rooms boast private balconies or patios, allowing you to enjoy stunning views of Sedona's iconic red rock formations.
- **In-Room Amenities:** Standard amenities include refrigerators, microwaves, and coffee makers for added convenience during your stay.

- **Family-Friendly Options:** Creekside villas offer additional space and amenities like full kitchens, perfect for families or groups traveling together.

Average Cost:

The average cost per night at Best Western Plus Arroyo Roble Hotel & Creekside Villas varies depending on the season, room type, and occupancy. Generally, rates are considered budget-friendly compared to other Sedona options, ranging from $100 to $300 per night.

Nearest Attraction:

- **Gallery Row:** Immerse yourself in Sedona's vibrant art scene with a stroll through Gallery Row, featuring a wide range of art galleries showcasing local and regional talent.

Nearest Restaurant:

- **Several Dining Options Nearby:** The hotel is located near a variety of restaurants offering diverse cuisines, from casual cafes to sit-down establishments. You're sure to find something to satisfy your cravings within walking distance.

Hotel Links and Contact:

- Website: https://www.bestwestern.com/en_US/book/hotels-in-sedona/best-western-plus-arroyo-roble-hotel-creekside-villas/propertyCode.03099.html
- Contact: (800) 780-7234

Location:

Best Western Plus Arroyo Roble Hotel & Creekside Villas is situated at 400 North State Route 89A, Sedona, Arizona 86336, USA.

Residence Inn by Marriott

Residence Inn by Marriott offers a convenient and stylish haven for travelers seeking a comfortable and flexible stay. This all-suite hotel caters to extended stays or those who prefer a touch of home away from home, perfect for families, groups, or business travelers.

About the Inn:

Residence Inn by Marriott Sedona prioritizes comfort and convenience. Spacious suites provide ample living areas, fully equipped kitchens, and modern amenities, allowing you to feel at ease and create a routine during your Sedona adventure. The friendly staff and relaxed atmosphere ensure an enjoyable stay.

Property Amenities:

- **Sparkling Outdoor Pool and Hot Tub:** Take a refreshing dip in the pool or unwind in the soothing hot tub after a day of exploration. Enjoy the Arizona sunshine and breathtaking red rock views while you relax.
- **Fitness Center:** Maintain your workout routine with access to the on-site fitness center featuring a variety of exercise equipment.
- **Complimentary Hot Breakfast Buffet:** Fuel your day with a delicious complimentary hot breakfast buffet, offering a wide selection of options to start your Sedona adventures.
- **Outdoor Grills and Fire Pit:** Enjoy a cookout under the stars with access to on-site barbecue grills and a fire pit. Perfect for a casual gathering or preparing meals during your stay.
- **Guest Laundry Facilities:** Take care of laundry needs with convenient

on-site guest laundry facilities.

- **Wireless Internet Access:** Stay connected with complimentary Wi-Fi throughout the property.
- **Free Parking:** Ample on-site parking is available for guests.

Room Features:

- **Spacious Suites:** Choose from a variety of studio, one-bedroom, or even two-bedroom suites, all offering ample space to relax and unwind.
- **Fully-Equipped Kitchens:** In-suite kitchens boast full-size appliances, cookware, and utensils, allowing you to prepare meals at your convenience.
- **Separate Living and Sleeping Areas:** The clear separation between living and sleeping areas provides a sense of normalcy and allows for relaxation during your stay.
- **Modern Amenities:** All suites come equipped with flat-screen TVs, premium cable channels, and comfortable furnishings for your comfort.
- **Private Balconies in Some Rooms:** Enjoy your morning coffee or an evening glass of wine on your private balcony, taking in the mesmerizing red rock vistas.

Average Cost:

The average cost per night at Residence Inn by Marriott Sedona varies from $200 - $400 per night.

Nearest Attraction:

- **Chapel of the Holy Cross:** Embark on a scenic drive or a short hike to reach this iconic landmark, a small chapel nestled amidst the red rocks, offering breathtaking views.

Nearest Restaurant:

- **Several Dining Options Nearby:** The hotel is situated near a variety of restaurants offering diverse cuisines, from casual cafes to sit-down establishments. You're sure to find something to satisfy your cravings within walking distance.

Hotel Links and Contact:

- Website: https://www.marriott.com/en-us/hotels/flgrs-residence-inn-sedona/overview/
- Contact: +1 928-239-7470

Location:

Residence Inn by Marriott Sedona is situated at 100 Thunder Mountain Road, Sedona, Arizona 86351, USA.

Arabella Hotel Sedona

Cradle yourself in the embrace of Sedona's iconic red rocks at Arabella Hotel. This award-winning resort promises an unforgettable stay with breathtaking scenery, personalized service, and a plethora of amenities for a truly rejuvenating experience.

About the Hotel:

Tucked away amidst eight acres of scenic Sedona landscape, Arabella Hotel exudes a relaxed and inviting atmosphere. The focus on local art and design creates a sense of place, while the friendly staff ensures a warm welcome and exceptional service. Whether you're seeking adventure or relaxation, Arabella Hotel provides the perfect haven.

Property Amenities:

- **Sweeping Red Rock Views:** Immerse yourself in the beauty of Sedona from the moment you arrive. Many guest areas and rooms boast captivating views of the red rock formations, adding a touch of magic to your stay.
- **Sparkling Pool and Scenic Overlook:** Take a refreshing dip in the pool or unwind on a chaise lounge, all while soaking in the breathtaking red rock vistas. The scenic overlook with comfortable seating offers a tranquil spot to relax and enjoy the sunset.
- **Arabella Bike Spa:** Gear up for adventure with Arabella's dedicated bike spa. This fully equipped facility provides bike washing stations, a repair station, and air pump, catering to both mountain bikers and road cyclists.
- **Complimentary Cruiser Bikes:** Explore Sedona's charm and nearby attractions with complimentary cruiser bikes available for guest use.
- **Concierge Services:** The knowledgeable concierge team is happy to assist you with activity planning, restaurant recommendations, and making the most of your Sedona experience.
- **Wireless Internet Access:** Stay connected with complimentary Wi-Fi throughout the property.
- **Free Parking:** On-site parking is available for guests.

Room Features:

- **Spacious Accommodations:** Choose from a variety of comfortable rooms and suites, all featuring modern furnishings and a warm ambiance.
- **Most Rooms with Red Rock Views:** Unwind on your private balcony or patio and marvel at the mesmerizing red rock formations, creating a truly unforgettable experience.
- **Custom Honeycomb Chairs:** Relax in style on the unique honeycomb chairs featured on most room patios or balconies, offering a comfortable

spot to enjoy the fresh air and scenery.

- **Modern Amenities:** In-room amenities include 42-inch HDTVs, USB charging stations, studio-size refrigerators, Keurig coffee makers, hairdryers, and custom bath amenities.

Average Cost:

The average cost per night at Arabella Hotel Sedona varies depending on the season, room type, and occupancy. Generally, rates range from $329 to upwards of $500 per night.

Nearest Attraction:

- **Tlaquepaque Arts and Shopping Village:** Immerse yourself in the vibrant arts and culture scene with a visit to Tlaquepaque, a charming village showcasing local and regional art galleries, handcrafted souvenirs, and delectable restaurants, all within walking distance.

Nearest Restaurant:

- **Twisted Vine Sedona:** Savor upscale American cuisine with a focus on fresh, seasonal ingredients at Twisted Vine, conveniently located within walking distance of the hotel. Enjoy stunning red rock views while indulging in a delicious meal.

Hotel Links and Contact:

- Website: https://www.arabellahotelsedona.com/
- Contact: (928) 963-1782

Location:

Arabella Hotel Sedona is situated at 1000 Airport Road, Sedona, Arizona 86351, USA.

Embark on an unforgettable Sedona adventure with Arabella Hotel as your base. With its stunning setting, exceptional service, and convenient location, this award-winning resort caters to discerning travelers seeking a luxurious and rejuvenating experience.

The Wilde Resort and Spa

This boutique resort beckons travelers seeking a haven of tranquility, luxurious accommodations, and a deep connection to Sedona's mystical energy.

About the Hotel:

The Wilde Resort and Spa embodies a philosophy of harmony with nature. Sustainable practices and a focus on wellness weave throughout the guest experience. Personalized service and a dedication to exceeding expectations ensure an unforgettable stay.

Property Amenities:

- **Outdoor Infinity Pool and Hot Tub:** Immerse yourself in the beauty of Sedona while unwinding in the sparkling infinity pool or soothing hot tub. Breathtaking red rock views enhance the sense of relaxation.
- **Wilde Haven Spa:** Indulge in a variety of rejuvenating spa treatments designed to nurture your body and mind. Experienced therapists offer massages, facials, and wellness rituals inspired by Sedona's healing traditions.
- **Fitness Center:** Maintain your workout routine with access to the well-equipped fitness center featuring modern exercise equipment.
- **Hiking and Biking Trails:** Explore Sedona's natural wonders directly

from the property. A network of scenic trails allows you to connect with the beauty of the red rocks.

- **Complimentary Yoga Classes:** Start your day with a complimentary yoga class, fostering mindfulness and inner peace amidst the Sedona landscape.
- **Stargazing Activities:** Unveil the magic of Sedona's night sky with guided stargazing sessions offered by the resort.
- **Concierge Services:** The knowledgeable concierge team is happy to assist you with activity planning, restaurant recommendations, and creating a personalized Sedona experience.
- **Wireless Internet Access:** Stay connected with complimentary Wi-Fi throughout the property.
- **Free Parking:** On-site parking is available for guests.

Room Features:

- **Luxurious Accommodations:** Choose from a variety of exquisitely designed rooms, suites, and even private villas, all offering unparalleled comfort and a sense of place.
- **Fireplaces and Private Balconies/Patios:** Cozy up by a crackling fireplace (available in most rooms) or relax on your private balcony or patio, taking in the breathtaking red rock views.
- **Deep Soaking Tubs:** Indulge in a rejuvenating soak in the luxurious deep soaking tubs featured in many rooms.
- **High-End Amenities:** Modern conveniences include premium bedding, plush bathrobes, Keurig coffee makers, and flat-screen TVs with cable channels.
- **Sustainable Practices:** The resort implements eco-friendly practices within the rooms, minimizing environmental impact while maintaining guest comfort.

Average Cost:

The average cost per night at The Wilde Resort and Spa rates range from $450 to upwards of $800 per night.

Nearest Attraction:

- **Thunder Mountain Trail:** Embark on a scenic hike directly from the property. Thunder Mountain Trail offers stunning red rock formations and panoramic views of Sedona.

Nearest Restaurant:

- **Elote Cafe:** Savor delectable Southwestern cuisine with a focus on fresh, local ingredients at Elote Cafe, located a short distance away.

Hotel Links and Contact:

- Website: https://www.tripadvisor.com/Hotel_Review-g31352-d55334 2-Reviews-The_Wilde_Resort_and_Spa-Sedona_Arizona.html
- Contact: (800) 249-3797

Location:
The Wilde Resort and Spa is situated at 300 Bluff Trail, Sedona, Arizona 86351, USA.

Sedona Real Inn & Suite

Sedona Real Inn & Suites invites you to experience Sedona's charm and natural wonders with a comfortable and affordable stay. This family-run hotel offers a warm atmosphere, convenient location, and a variety of amenities ideal for exploring the beauty of Sedona.

About the Hotel:

Established in 1962, Sedona Real Inn & Suites maintains a traditional Southwestern aesthetic, prioritizing comfort and hospitality. The friendly staff ensures a welcoming environment, making it a perfect basecamp for your Sedona adventure.

Property Amenities:

- **Outdoor Pool and Spa:** Relax after a day of exploration in the sparkling, seasonally heated pool or unwind in the jacuzzi, surrounded by Sedona's red rock landscape.
- **Landscaped Grounds with Patios:** Stroll through the well-maintained grounds featuring native plants and colorful flowers. Relax on the patios and soak in the sunshine or enjoy a cup of coffee amidst the fresh air.
- **Complimentary Hot Breakfast Buffet:** Start your day with a delicious complimentary hot breakfast buffet offering a selection of pastries, cereals, fruits, and beverages.
- **Barbecue Grills and Picnic Area:** Enjoy an outdoor meal with access to on-site barbecue grills and picnic tables. Perfect for a casual gathering or a cookout under the stars.
- **Wireless Internet Access:** Stay connected with complimentary Wi-Fi throughout the property.
- **Free Parking:** On-site parking is available for guests.
- **Pet-Friendly Accommodations:** Looking to bring your furry companion? Sedona Real Inn & Suites welcomes well-behaved pets with a dedicated dog play area and waste disposal stations.

Room Features:

- **Comfortable Accommodations:** Choose from a variety of rooms, all offering a cozy and comfortable atmosphere.

- **Private Balconies or Patios (Some Rooms):** Unwind on your private balcony or patio (available in select rooms) and enjoy the fresh air or take in the views of the surrounding landscape.
- **Refrigerators and Microwaves:** In-room amenities like refrigerators and microwaves provide added convenience for storing drinks and snacks or preparing light meals.
- **Coffee Makers:** Start your day with a cup of coffee brewed in the convenience of your room.
- **Traditional Furnishings:** The rooms feature a traditional Southwestern style with comfortable furnishings and warm color palettes.

Average Cost:

The average cost per night at Sedona Real Inn & Suites varies depending on the season, room type, and occupancy. Generally, rates are considered budget-friendly compared to other Sedona properties, ranging from $106 to $300 per night.

Nearest Attraction:

- **Bell Rock:** This iconic red rock formation, a short drive from the hotel, offers scenic views and hiking trails suitable for all skill levels. Capture stunning photographs of this natural landmark.

Nearest Restaurant:

- **The Hideaway House:** Located within walking distance, The Hideaway House offers a casual dining experience with a focus on American comfort food and local ingredients.

Hotel Links and Contact:

- Website: https://www.sedonareal.com/
- Contact: (928) 282-3371

Location:

Sedona Real Inn & Suites is situated at 505 West State Route 89A, Sedona, Arizona 86351, USA.

Amara Resort and Spa

This luxurious hotel caters to discerning travelers seeking a blend of comfort, exceptional service, and a plethora of amenities, all designed to create a rejuvenating experience.

About the Hotel:

Amara Resort and Spa reflects the essence of Sedona, seamlessly integrating contemporary design with the natural beauty of the surroundings. Spacious accommodations, personalized attention to detail, and a focus on wellness ensure a truly relaxing and unforgettable escape.

Property Amenities:

- **Heated Infinity Pool and Hot Tub:** Indulge in the beauty of Sedona while unwinding in the sparkling infinity pool or soothing hot tub. Take in breathtaking red rock views as you soak and relax.
- **Award-Winning Amara Spa:** Pamper yourself with a variety of rejuvenating spa treatments designed to nurture your body and mind. Choose from massages, facials, body wraps, and other therapeutic offerings in a tranquil environment.
- **SaltRock Kitchen:** Embark on a culinary adventure at the hotel's

signature restaurant, SaltRock Kitchen. Savor innovative dishes prepared with fresh, local ingredients, complemented by stunning pool views.

- **State-of-the-Art Fitness Center:** Maintain your workout routine with access to the well-equipped fitness center featuring modern exercise equipment.
- **Yoga Classes:** Unwind and find inner peace with complimentary yoga classes offered on-site.
- **Free Bicycle Rentals:** Explore Sedona's scenic trails and charming streets with complimentary bicycle rentals available for guests.
- **Gift Shop:** Browse through a curated selection of souvenirs, Sedona-themed gifts, and essentials at the on-site gift shop.
- **Concierge Services:** The knowledgeable concierge team is happy to assist you with activity planning, restaurant recommendations, and making the most of your Sedona experience.
- **Wireless Internet Access:** Stay connected with complimentary Wi-Fi throughout the property.
- **Free Parking:** On-site parking is available for guests.
- **Pet-Friendly Accommodations (with fees):** Looking to bring your furry companion? Amara Resort offers pet-friendly accommodations with designated fees.

Room Features:

- **Spacious Accommodations:** Unwind in luxurious guest rooms or suites, all featuring plush furnishings, private balconies or patios, and ample space for relaxation.
- **Breathtaking Red Rock Views (most rooms):** Immerse yourself in the beauty of Sedona with stunning red rock vistas visible from most rooms.
- **In-Room Amenities:** Modern conveniences include premium bedding, flat-screen TVs with cable channels, iHome docking stations for your devices, and luxurious C.O. Bigelow bath amenities.
- **Coffee Service:** Start your day with a cup of coffee brewed in the

convenience of your room with the in-room Illy coffee service.

Average Cost:

The average cost per night at Amara Resort and Spa rates range from $400 to upwards of $1,000 per night.

Nearest Attraction:

- **Oak Creek Canyon:** Explore the stunning scenery of Oak Creek Canyon, a short drive from the hotel. Hike along scenic trails, take a jeep tour, or cool off with a refreshing dip in the creek.

Nearest Restaurant:

- **SaltRock Kitchen:** For a convenient and delectable dining experience, the on-site SaltRock Kitchen offers innovative Southwestern cuisine prepared with fresh, seasonal ingredients.

Hotel Links and Contact:

- Website: https://www.amararesort.com/
- Contact: (928) 282-3300

Location:

Amara Resort and Spa is situated at 100 Amara Lane, Sedona, Arizona 86351, USA.

Enchantment Resort:

About the Resort:

Enchantment Resort embodies a philosophy of connection with nature. Spacious accommodations seamlessly blend with the surrounding landscape, while personalized attention and a dedication to exceeding expectations ensure an unforgettable stay. Whether you crave outdoor adventure or pure relaxation, Enchantment Resort provides the perfect haven.

Property Amenities:

- **Multiple Pools and Hot Tubs:** Choose from two sparkling pools, one catering to families and another offering an adults-only escape. Unwind in the soothing hot tubs after a day of exploration, all while soaking in the red rock views.
- **Mii amo Spa:** Indulge in a variety of rejuvenating spa treatments designed to nurture your body and mind at the award-winning Mii amo Spa. Experienced therapists offer massages, facials, and wellness rituals inspired by Sedona's healing traditions.
- **Award-Winning Dining:** Embark on a culinary journey at Enchantment Resort's exceptional restaurants. Savor creative dishes featuring fresh, local ingredients, complemented by stunning red rock vistas.
- **Trail House:** This epicenter for outdoor adventures offers guided hikes, mountain bike rentals, and expert advice on exploring Sedona's vast trail network. Stop by the Trail House store for the latest outdoor gear and apparel.
- **Complimentary Activities:** Enjoy a variety of complimentary activities offered by the resort, including guided nature walks, stargazing sessions, and fitness classes.
- **Concierge Services:** The knowledgeable concierge team is happy to assist you with activity planning, restaurant recommendations, and creating a personalized Sedona experience.
- **Wireless Internet Access:** Stay connected with complimentary Wi-Fi

throughout the property.

- **Valet and Self-Parking Options:** Choose between convenient valet parking or self-parking options for your vehicle.
- **Pet-Friendly Accommodations (with fees):** Looking to bring your furry companion? Enchantment Resort offers pet-friendly accommodations with designated fees and walking trails.

Room Features:

- **Upscale Accommodations:** Choose from a variety of luxurious casitas, suites, and even private villas, all offering stunning red rock views, private balconies or patios, and ample space for relaxation.
- **Fireplaces and Soaking Tubs:** Cozy up by a crackling fireplace (available in most rooms) and unwind in a deep soaking tub, creating a truly rejuvenating experience.
- **High-End Amenities:** Modern conveniences include plush furnishings, premium bedding, flat-screen TVs with cable channels, and luxurious bath amenities.
- **Outdoor Living Spaces:** Unwind on your private balcony or patio, breathe in the fresh air, and marvel at the mesmerizing red rock scenery.

Average Cost:

The average cost per night rates range from $400 to upwards of $1,000 per night.

Nearest Attraction:

- **Chimney Rock:** Hike or drive to the iconic Chimney Rock formation, towering right behind the resort. Capture stunning photographs and explore the scenic trails surrounding this natural landmark.

Nearest Restaurant:

- **Enchantment Resort Restaurants:** For a convenient and delectable dining experience, Enchantment Resort boasts award-winning restaurants featuring innovative dishes prepared with fresh, local ingredients.

Hotel Links and Contact:

- Website: https://www.enchantmentresort.com/
- Contact: (928) 282-3300

Location:

Enchantment Resort is situated at 100 Eckert Road, Sedona, Arizona 86351, USA.

Vacation Rental

Tiny Camp Sedona

Tiny Camp Sedona offers a unique and unforgettable way to experience the magic of Sedona, Arizona. Immerse yourself in nature's beauty with a stay in one of their tastefully designed tiny homes, perfect for couples, solo adventurers, or minimalist travelers seeking a comfortable and eco-friendly lodging option.

Overview:

Tiny Camp Sedona provides a collection of handcrafted tiny homes, each thoughtfully designed to maximize comfort and functionality within a compact space. These charming accommodations blend seamlessly with the surrounding red rock landscape, allowing you to connect with nature without sacrificing modern amenities.

Condo/Apartment:

While Tiny Camp Sedona technically doesn't offer traditional condos or apartments, their tiny homes provide a cozy and self-contained living space. Each tiny home is meticulously designed to feel like a miniature home, complete with a sleeping area, bathroom, kitchenette, and living space.

House Rules:

- **Respectful Occupancy:** Tiny Camp Sedona prioritizes a peaceful and respectful environment for all guests.
- **Maximum Occupancy:** The number of guests allowed varies depending on the specific tiny home you book. Be sure to confirm occupancy limits when making your reservation.
- **No Smoking:** Smoking is strictly prohibited inside the tiny homes and on the property.
- **Pet Policy:** Tiny Camp Sedona has a variable pet policy depending on the specific tiny home. Some tiny homes may be pet-friendly with prior approval and additional fees. Always check before bringing your furry companion.
- **Quiet Hours:** Respect the tranquility of the surroundings by observing quiet hours from 10 pm to 8 am.
- **Cleanliness:** Guests are expected to leave the tiny home clean upon departure. Basic cleaning supplies are provided.

Bathroom:

The tiny homes at Tiny Camp Sedona typically feature compact but well-appointed bathrooms. These may include a toilet, sink, and a shower stall. Linens and towels are generally provided.

Bedroom:

Sleeping arrangements vary depending on the specific tiny home. Some may offer a queen-size bed or a comfortable murphy bed that folds away when not in use. Bedding linens are typically provided.

Amenities and Things to Know:

- **Kitchenette:** Prepare light meals or heat up leftovers in the well-equipped kitchenette, featuring a mini fridge, microwave, and basic cookware.
- **Fire Pit (most tiny homes):** Cozy up under the stars and roast marshmallows by the fire pit available in most tiny homes. Firewood

may be available for purchase.

- **Deck or Patio (most tiny homes):** Relax and enjoy the fresh air on the private deck or patio overlooking the red rock scenery. Some decks may have seating and a small table.
- **Limited Electronics:** Tiny Camp Sedona emphasizes a connection with nature. While some tiny homes may have a small TV or DVD player, cellphone reception can be limited in the area.
- **Wireless Internet:** Wi-Fi may or may not be available depending on the specific tiny home. Inquire at the time of booking.
- **Limited Storage Space:** Due to the compact nature of the tiny homes, storage space is limited. Pack light and bring only essentials.

Sedona Self-Love Retreats

Overview:

Sedona Self-Love Retreats specializes in personalized wellness retreats designed to foster self-discovery, mindfulness, and inner peace. They focus on individual journeys, providing comfortable and private accommodations within a supportive environment.

Accommodations:

Sedona Self-Love Retreats may utilize various accommodations depending on the specific retreat program. These could include private rooms within a retreat center, individual cabins, or even glamping options (luxury camping) surrounded by Sedona's natural beauty.

House Rules:

House rules at Sedona Self-Love Retreats will likely prioritize a peaceful and supportive environment conducive to self-reflection and relaxation. General guidelines might include:

- **Respectful Conduct:** Respect fellow participants and the retreat facilitators.
- **Minimal Disruptions:** Minimize noise and distractions to ensure everyone can fully embrace the retreat experience.
- **Curtailed Electronics:** Some retreats may encourage limited phone and electronic usage to promote mindfulness and disconnection from daily routines.
- **Healthy Habits:** Maintaining a healthy lifestyle is often encouraged during self-love retreats, with guidelines on nutritious meals, exercise, and sleep schedules (depending on the program).
- **Confidentiality:** Respect the privacy and confidentiality of fellow participants during group sessions or discussions.

Bathroom and Bedroom:

The specific configuration of bathrooms and bedrooms will vary depending on the retreat venue and the type of accommodation provided (private room, cabin, glamping). However, you can generally expect clean and comfortable facilities that prioritize relaxation.

Amenities and Things to Know:

- **Self-Love Focused Activities:** The core element of Sedona Self-Love Retreats revolves around guided activities, workshops, and sessions designed to promote self-discovery, mindfulness, and emotional well-being. These may include yoga, meditation, journaling exercises, breathwork, or art therapy (depending on the program).
- **Healthy Meals:** Many retreats include delicious and nutritious meals prepared with fresh ingredients, often catering to dietary restrictions.
- **Stunning Surroundings:** Immerse yourself in the beauty of Sedona's red rocks and natural landscapes, creating a perfect backdrop for your self-love journey.
- **Limited Wi-Fi:** Some retreats may have limited or restricted Wi-Fi

access to encourage digital detox and focus on self-connection.

- **Group vs. Individual Retreats:** Sedona Self-Love Retreats may offer group retreats or personalized individual programs. Choose the option that best suits your needs and preferences.

Sycamore Springs Guest House:

Sycamore Springs Guest House offers a cozy and welcoming haven for travelers seeking a comfortable and affordable stay in Sedona, Arizona. This charming bed and breakfast provides a unique alternative to traditional hotels, fostering a sense of community and connection with other guests and the friendly.

Overview:

Sycamore Springs Guest House exudes a warm and inviting atmosphere. The historic building, potentially with a rich history, is likely surrounded by beautiful Sedona scenery. The innkeepers prioritize hospitality and ensure a comfortable and memorable stay. Whether you're a solo adventurer, a couple seeking a romantic getaway, or a small group of friends exploring Sedona, Sycamore Springs Guest House offers a delightful place to unwind and recharge.

Condo/Apartment:

Sycamore Springs Guest House doesn't typically offer condo or apartment-style accommodations. This is a bed and breakfast, meaning guests typically rent individual rooms within the main house or a potentially attached guest wing.

House Rules:

House rules at Sycamore Springs Guest House will likely promote a peaceful and respectful environment for all guests. Here are some general expectations:

- **Check-In and Check-Out Times:** Be mindful of designated check-in and check-out times to ensure a smooth transition for all guests.
- **Shared Spaces:** Respect common areas like the living room, dining room, or garden, keeping noise levels reasonable and being courteous to other guests.
- **Courtesy:** Maintain cleanliness in shared bathrooms and be mindful of others' needs when using shared amenities.
- **No Smoking:** Smoking is likely prohibited inside the guest house and potentially outdoors as well. Designated smoking areas may be available, inquire with the innkeepers.
- **Quiet Hours:** Respect the tranquility of the environment by observing designated quiet hours, typically during the evenings and early mornings.

Bathroom and Bedroom:

The configuration of bathrooms and bedrooms will vary depending on the specific room you reserve. Some rooms may have en-suite bathrooms, while others may share a bathroom with a limited number of guests. The bedrooms will likely offer comfortable beds, quality linens, and closet space for your belongings.

Amenities and Things to Know:

- **Breakfast:** A delicious and complimentary breakfast is often a highlight of a stay at a bed and breakfast. Sycamore Springs Guest House might offer a homemade breakfast featuring local ingredients and catering to various dietary needs (check details when booking).
- **Common Areas:** Relax and unwind in comfortable common areas like a living room with plush sofas and potentially a fireplace, a dining room for shared meals, or a beautiful garden for enjoying the fresh air.
- **Limited Kitchen Access:** While not a full condo/apartment, some guest

houses may offer a shared kitchen or kitchenette for basic needs like preparing coffee or light snacks. Inquire with the innkeepers about the availability and usage guidelines.

- **Limited Laundry Facilities:** Laundry facilities may be available on-site or nearby. Inquire with the innkeepers about laundry options and any associated fees.
- **Local Recommendations:** The innkeepers are likely a wealth of knowledge about Sedona and can provide personalized recommendations for restaurants, attractions, and activities to create a memorable itinerary for your stay.

Unveiling Luxury at Sedona Penthouse

Sedona Penthouse beckons discerning travelers seeking an unparalleled experience in the heart of Sedona, Arizona. This luxurious penthouse condo promises breathtaking red rock views, high-end amenities, and a private haven for your unforgettable Sedona escape.

Overview:

Perched atop a stylish building (potentially with a name or location hint), Sedona Penthouse offers a one-of-a-kind accommodation. This spacious condo provides the comfort and privacy of a home with the convenience of condo living. Imagine waking up to mesmerizing red rock vistas, unwinding in a private balcony, and indulging in luxurious amenities – Sedona Penthouse promises an unforgettable stay.

Condo/Apartment:

Sedona Penthouse falls under the condo/apartment category. However, unlike a typical condo unit, it occupies the entire penthouse floor, offering a sense of exclusivity and unparalleled views.

House Rules:

House rules at Sedona Penthouse will likely ensure a peaceful and enjoyable experience for all residents:

- **Maximum Occupancy:** The penthouse will have a designated maximum occupancy limit. Ensure your group size adheres to this limit for comfort and safety.
- **No Smoking:** Smoking is likely prohibited inside the penthouse and potentially on balconies or patios.
- **Noise Restrictions:** Respect the tranquility of the building by adhering to designated quiet hours, typically during nighttime hours.
- **Parking:** Inquire about parking options at the time of booking. The penthouse may have a designated parking space in the building's garage or assigned outdoor parking.
- **Trash Removal:** Follow the building's guidelines for trash disposal to maintain a clean and pleasant environment.

Bathroom and Bedroom:

The exact configuration may vary, but Sedona Penthouse is likely to boast:

- **Multiple Bathrooms:** Expect multiple luxurious bathrooms with showers, bathtubs (potentially jetted tubs for an extra touch of indulgence), and high-quality toiletries.
- **Spacious Bedrooms:** The penthouse will likely have multiple bedrooms, each featuring comfortable beds, plush linens, and ample closet space. Sleeping arrangements may include king-size beds, queen-size beds, or a combination depending on the layout.

Amenities and Things to Know:

- **Breathtaking Views:** The pièce de résistance of Sedona Penthouse is undoubtedly the captivating red rock vista visible from expansive windows, balconies, or a private rooftop terrace (depending on the specific features).

- **Gourmet Kitchen:** Prepare delicious meals in a well-equipped gourmet kitchen featuring modern appliances, granite countertops, and high-quality cookware.
- **Living Room for Entertainment:** Relax and unwind in a spacious living room with plush sofas, a fireplace (potentially), a large flat-screen TV with cable or satellite channels, and potentially a game room or entertainment area.
- **Balcony or Rooftop Terrace:** Step outside and soak in the fresh air and stunning scenery from a private balcony or rooftop terrace, perfect for morning coffee, evening drinks, or al fresco dining.
- **High-Speed Wi-Fi:** Stay connected with complimentary high-speed Wi-Fi throughout your stay.
- **In-Unit Laundry:** Enjoy the convenience of in-unit laundry facilities, allowing you to pack light and easily refresh your belongings during your stay.
- **Security Deposit:** A security deposit may be required to cover any potential damages during your stay. The amount will be refunded upon check-out if no damages occur.

Must- Try Cuisine

Latin-Inspired Grilled Meats

Latin America boasts a vibrant grilling culture, and grilled meats are a cornerstone of many culinary traditions. Here's a glimpse into the world of Latin-inspired grilled meats, exploring the ingredients, preparation methods, and the explosion of flavors they deliver.

Ingredients:

The beauty of Latin-inspired grilled meats lies in their simplicity. The primary ingredient is, of course, the meat. Popular choices include:

- **Beef:** Skirt steak (flank steak), ribeye, New York strip, and tri-tip are all excellent options.
- **Chicken:** Whole chickens, bone-in breasts, thighs, or wings are all perfect for grilling.
- **Seafood:** Shrimp, skewered fish like mahi-mahi or swordfish, and even octopus are popular choices in some regions.

Preparation:

Marinades are where the Latin magic happens. Aromatic spices, citrus juices, and fresh herbs create flavor profiles that are both complex and mouthwatering. Common ingredients include:

- **Spices:** Achiote paste, cumin, chili powder, oregano, and adobo seasoning are staples. Guajillo, ancho, and chipotle peppers add smokiness and heat.
- **Acids:** Fresh lime juice, orange juice, and even sour orange (naranja agria) add a tangy brightness that balances richer flavors.
- **Fresh Herbs:** Cilantro, parsley, garlic, and sofrito (a base of sauteed onions, peppers, and herbs) infuse the meats with fresh aromatics.

The meats are typically marinated for several hours, allowing the flavors to penetrate deeply. Some preparations involve slow-cooking the marinated meat partially before grilling to ensure tenderness.

The Savor:

The first bite of a perfectly grilled Latin-inspired meat is an explosion of flavor. The smoky char from the grill mingles with the complex notes from the marinade. Tenderness gives way to juicy richness, and the tangy acidity provides a delightful counterpoint. The specific flavor profile varies depending on the chosen spices and herbs. Achiote paste lends a warm, earthy touch, while adobo seasoning brings a smoky guajillo pepper punch. Fresh herbs like cilantro add a bright, citrusy note.

The Latin Flair:

Latin-inspired grilled meats aren't just about the taste; they're about the experience. The sizzling sounds on the grill, the vibrant colors of the marinades, and the aroma of spices wafting through the air all contribute to a lively and festive atmosphere. These grilled meats are often served alongside accompaniments like rice, beans, grilled vegetables, and fresh tortillas, making them a complete and satisfying meal perfect for sharing with friends and family.

So, next time you fire up the grill, consider adding a Latin twist to your repertoire. With simple ingredients, flavorful marinades, and the magic of grilling, you can create a culinary adventure that will tantalize your taste buds and transport you to the heart of Latin America.

Fresh Seafood

Fresh seafood offers a unique and delectable dining experience. Unlike land animals, seafood absorbs the flavors of the ocean, resulting in a clean, briny taste unlike anything else.

Ingredients:

The beauty of fresh seafood lies in its simplicity. The star of the show is, of course, the catch itself. Popular choices include:

- **Finfish:** Salmon, tuna, cod, halibut, mahi-mahi, snapper, and countless others, each with its own unique texture and flavor profile.
- **Shellfish:** Shrimp, prawns, lobster, crab, oysters, clams, mussels – the bounty of the ocean offers a vast array of shellfish options.

Beyond the main catch, some additional ingredients might be used depending on the preparation method:

- **Fresh Herbs:** Lemon wedges, dill, parsley, cilantro, and chives often accompany seafood dishes, adding brightness and freshness.
- **Acids:** Lemon juice, lime juice, and even white wine are used to enhance the natural flavors and add a touch of acidity.
- **Fats:** Butter, olive oil, and sometimes even avocado oil are used for cooking or drizzled on top for added richness.
- **Spices:** Depending on the recipe, minimal spices like black pepper, Old Bay seasoning, or Cajun spice blends might be used to complement the natural flavors.

Preparation:

The preparation methods for fresh seafood are as diverse as the ocean itself. Here are some popular techniques:

- **Simple Searing:** A quick sear on a hot pan or grill creates a beautiful crust while leaving the interior perfectly cooked and juicy.
- **Baking:** This gentle cooking method is perfect for delicate fish like cod or flaky salmon.
- **Poaching:** Submerging seafood in simmering liquid allows for gentle cooking and preserves the delicate flavors and textures.
- **Steaming:** Another gentle approach that retains moisture and nutrients, ideal for shellfish and some finfish varieties.
- **Grilling:** Imparts a smoky flavor and beautiful grill marks, perfect for heartier fish like tuna steaks or swordfish.

The Savor:

The first bite of fresh seafood is a delightful experience. The texture can vary depending on the species, ranging from the firm flesh of a seared tuna steak to the delicate flakiness of cooked cod. The prevalent flavor is a clean, briny essence of the ocean, unlike any land animal protein. Depending on the preparation, additional flavor notes emerge. A simple sear highlights the natural sweetness of the fish, while a lemon butter sauce adds a touch of tangy richness.

The Flavor Symphony:

Fresh seafood offers a symphony of flavors on the palate. The inherent briny taste is the foundation, but it's beautifully complemented by other elements. A squeeze of lemon juice enhances the natural sweetness, while fresh herbs like dill or cilantro add a pop of brightness. Spices like black pepper or Cajun seasoning can introduce a touch of warmth or heat. Cooking methods like searing or grilling contribute a smoky char, adding another layer of complexity.

The Essence of Freshness:

The key to enjoying fresh seafood is appreciating its inherent qualities. Simple preparations that highlight the natural flavors and textures are often the most rewarding. With a variety of preparation methods and endless flavor combinations to explore, fresh seafood offers a culinary adventure for every palate. So next time you're looking for a light, healthy, and delicious meal, consider the bounty of the ocean and savor the symphony of flavors that fresh seafood offers.

Wood-Fired Pizza

Wood-fired pizza is a culinary masterpiece, a delightful dance between simple ingredients, fiery heat, and explosive flavor. Here's a look at what makes wood-fired pizza so special, from its essential components to the delightful experience of each savory bite.

Ingredients:

Wood-fired pizza relies on a core set of ingredients, each playing a crucial role:

- **Dough:** The foundation of any pizza, wood-fired varieties typically use a high-hydration dough. This creates a crispy crust with a satisfying chew and a slightly smoky flavor from the wood fire.
- **Tomato Sauce:** A quality tomato sauce forms the base for the toppings. San Marzano tomatoes are a popular choice, offering a balance of sweetness and acidity.
- **Cheese:** Mozzarella is the king of wood-fired pizzas, providing a creamy texture and a beautiful stretch when pulled. Additional cheeses like parmesan or ricotta can be added for extra richness and flavor.
- **Toppings:** This is where creativity shines! From classic options like pepperoni, sausage, and vegetables to gourmet choices like truffle oil and burrata, the topping possibilities are endless.

Preparation:

The magic of wood-fired pizza lies in the cooking method. Here's the process:

1. **Dough Stretching:** The pizzaiolo (pizza maker) skillfully stretches the dough by hand, creating a thin and airy crust.
2. **Toppings Assembly:** The chosen toppings are carefully arranged on the stretched dough, ensuring a balanced distribution of flavors and textures.
3. **Wood-Fired Oven:** The pizza is then loaded onto a peel (a long wooden paddle) and expertly maneuvered into the blazing wood-fired oven.
4. **High-Heat Cooking:** The intense heat of the wood fire, typically reaching upwards of 800°F (425°C), cooks the pizza quickly. This creates a beautifully blistered crust with a smoky char and perfectly melted cheese.

The Savor:

The first bite of a wood-fired pizza is a sensory experience. The visual appeal is undeniable – a slightly charred crust, bubbling cheese, and vibrant toppings. The aroma is intoxicating, a blend of smoky char, yeasty dough, and the enticing fragrance of the specific toppings. The first bite delivers a delightful textural contrast – the crispiness of the crust gives way to the soft chew of the dough, and the melted cheese adds a creamy richness.

The Flavor Explosion:

Wood-fired pizza offers a symphony of flavors on the palate. The smoky char from the wood fire infuses the crust with a unique taste that complements the natural sweetness of the dough. The tomato sauce provides a tangy base, while the cheese adds a salty and creamy element. Each bite bursts with the individual flavors of the chosen toppings, creating a harmonious and satisfying flavor profile.

Beyond the Basics:

While classic wood-fired pizzas are a delight, there's room for exploration. Pizzas "bianche" (white pizzas) forgo the tomato sauce, allowing the flavor of the dough and cheese to shine. Regional variations abound, with specific toppings and cooking styles reflecting local traditions.

The Allure of Wood-Fired Pizza:

The beauty of wood-fired pizza lies in its simplicity and versatility. Using high-quality ingredients and the magic of a wood-fired oven, pizzas become more than just a meal; they're a culinary experience that tantalizes the senses and satisfies the soul. So next time you crave a delicious and satisfying meal, consider the allure of wood-fired pizza and embark on a delightful journey of fire and flavor.

Homemade Pasta: A Labor of Love, a Symphony of Flavor

Homemade pasta is more than just a meal; it's a culinary journey that starts with simple ingredients and transforms into a delightful expression of taste and texture. Here's a glimpse into the world of homemade pasta, exploring its essential components, the preparation process, the delightful savor of each bite, and the multifaceted flavors it can offer.

Ingredients:

At its core, homemade pasta requires only a few basic ingredients:

- **Flour:** High-quality semolina flour or all-purpose flour are the most common choices. Semolina flour, made from durum wheat, creates a firmer and chewier pasta with a slightly nutty flavor. All-purpose flour offers a good balance of texture and flavor.
- **Eggs:** Eggs bind the dough ingredients together and contribute to the richness and color of the pasta.
- **Water:** The amount of water used is crucial for achieving the right dough consistency, which should be elastic and smooth.
- **Olive Oil (Optional):** A drizzle of olive oil can add a touch of richness and improve the dough's handling properties.

Preparation:

The preparation of homemade pasta is a therapeutic process:

1. **Mixing:** The dry ingredients, flour and a pinch of salt, are formed into a mound on a clean surface. Eggs are then added to a well in the center, and the ingredients are gradually incorporated to form a rough dough.
2. **Kneading:** The dough is kneaded for several minutes, either by hand or with a stand mixer. This process develops the gluten structure, resulting in a smooth and elastic dough.
3. **Resting:** The kneaded dough is wrapped in plastic wrap and allowed to rest for at least 30 minutes. This allows the gluten to relax, making the dough easier to roll out.
4. **Rolling:** The dough is rolled out into thin sheets using a rolling pin or a pasta machine. The thickness of the sheets will vary depending on the desired type of pasta – thin sheets for delicate ravioli or thicker sheets for lasagna.
5. **Shaping:** Once rolled out, the pasta sheets are cut into desired shapes using a knife, pasta cutters, or specialized molds. Common shapes include fettuccine, spaghetti, tagliatelle, or ravioli fillings.
6. **Cooking:** Fresh pasta cooks much faster than dried pasta varieties. Typically, 2-3 minutes of boiling salted water are enough to achieve perfectly al dente pasta.

The Savor:

The first bite of homemade pasta is a revelation. The texture is unlike store-bought varieties. It has a delightful springiness and a slight chewiness that comes from the fresh ingredients and the development of the gluten during kneading. The surface is slightly rough, allowing sauces to cling beautifully.

The Flavor Symphony:

Homemade pasta offers a blank canvas for a symphony of flavors. The subtle flavor of the wheat flour forms the foundation, but it readily absorbs the essence of sauces. A simple tomato sauce allows the natural sweetness of the wheat to shine, while a rich ragu adds depth and complexity. Fresh herbs like basil or parsley can add a touch of brightness, and cheeses like parmesan or ricotta provide a salty and creamy counterpoint.

Beyond the Basics:

The beauty of homemade pasta lies in its versatility. You can explore different flours for unique flavor profiles. Adding spinach puree to the dough creates vibrant green pasta, while incorporating herbs like rosemary or black peppercorns adds a subtle touch of flavor. The possibilities for fillings and sauces are endless, allowing you to create customized pasta dishes that reflect your personal taste.

The Reward of Homemade:

While store-bought pasta offers convenience, homemade pasta is an experience in itself. The act of kneading the dough, rolling it out, and shaping it into perfect forms is a form of culinary therapy. And the reward? A plate of pasta bursting with flavor and texture, a testament to the love and care put into its creation. So next time you're looking for a satisfying and rewarding culinary adventure, consider diving into the world of homemade pasta.

Elote (Mexican Street Corn)

Elote, also known as Mexican street corn, is a vibrant and flavorful side dish that tantalizes taste buds with its contrasting textures and symphony of sweet, savory, and spicy notes. Here's a look at what makes elote so special, from its simple ingredients to the delightful experience of each bite.

Ingredients:

Elote relies on a handful of fresh ingredients that come together beautifully:

- **Corn on the cob:** Freshly husked corn on the cob is the star of the show. Choose sweet corn at its peak for optimal flavor.

- **Mayonnaise:** This creamy base adds richness and helps bind the other ingredients to the corn.
- **Cotija cheese:** This salty, crumbly Mexican cheese provides a delightful contrast to the sweetness of the corn. Queso fresco can be substituted if Cotija is unavailable.
- **Chili powder:** Smoky and earthy chili powder adds a touch of warmth and depth of flavor.
- **Lime juice:** Fresh lime juice adds a burst of tangy acidity, balancing the richness of the mayonnaise and cheese.
- **Cilantro:** Fresh cilantro leaves bring a vibrant pop of freshness with their citrusy and herbaceous aroma.

Preparation:

The beauty of elote lies in its simplicity:

1. **Cooking the Corn:** The corn can be cooked in several ways – grilled, boiled, or roasted. Grilling adds a smoky char, while boiling or roasting keeps the corn nice and juicy.
2. **Spreading the Mayonnaise:** Spread a generous amount of mayonnaise over the cooked corn cob, ensuring even coverage.
3. **Seasoning:** Sprinkle chili powder and a pinch of salt over the mayonnaise-coated corn.
4. **Adding the Finishing Touches:** Crumble Cotija cheese over the corn, followed by a generous squeeze of fresh lime juice. Finally, top it all off with chopped fresh cilantro.

The Savor:

The first bite of elote is an explosion of textures and flavors. The warm, juicy corn kernels provide a satisfying chew. The creamy mayonnaise adds richness, while the crumbly Cotija cheese offers a salty counterpoint. The chili powder brings a touch of smokiness, beautifully balanced by the tangy brightness of the lime juice. Fresh cilantro adds a final touch of freshness with its herbaceous aroma.

The Flavor Symphony:

Elote offers a symphony of flavors on the palate. The inherent sweetness of the corn forms the base, but it's beautifully complemented by the other ingredients. The richness of the mayonnaise and the saltiness of the cheese create a delightful contrast. Chili powder adds a touch of warmth and smokiness, while the lime juice provides a burst of tanginess that cuts through the richness. Fresh cilantro's herbaceousness adds another layer of complexity, making each bite a delightful exploration of sweet, savory, spicy, and refreshing notes.

Beyond the Basics:

While the classic elote recipe is a crowd-pleaser, there's room for exploration. You can add a kick of heat with a sprinkle of cayenne pepper or a drizzle of sriracha. For a smoky twist, consider using chipotle powder instead of regular chili powder. Feeling adventurous? Try incorporating crumbled bacon or crumbled chorizo for added savory depth.

A Street Food Delight:

Elote is more than just a side dish; it's a street food experience. The vibrant colors, the inviting aroma, and the symphony of flavors in each bite make it a delightful representation of Mexican cuisine. So next time you're craving a satisfying and flavorful treat, look no further than elote, a testament to the beauty of simple ingredients and bold flavors.

Recommended Restaurant

Tortas de Fuego West Sedona

About:

Tortas de Fuego West Sedona is a family-owned restaurant serving up delicious and authentic Mexican cuisine. Established in 2011, they've grown from a home-based eatery to a well-regarded spot amongst Sedona's restaurant scene. They bring the rich flavors of Mexico City to the heart of West Sedona.

Food and Ambiance:

At Tortas de Fuego, expect a casual and counter-serve dining experience. The vibrant atmosphere and friendly service make it a welcoming spot to savor a taste of Mexico. Their menu features a variety of traditional Mexican favorites, perfect for a quick bite or a relaxed meal.

Cuisine:

Mexican. They specialize in tacos, tortas (Mexican sandwiches on soft rolls), and other traditional dishes like tostadas and burritos. Fresh ingredients and bold flavors are the hallmarks of their cuisine.

Price Range:

Tortas de Fuego offers a moderate price range. Expect to pay around $10-$19 for most entrees. This makes it a budget-friendly option for enjoying authentic Mexican food in Sedona.

Location and Contact:

- Address: 3190 West State Route 89A, Suite 550, Sedona, AZ 86336 (Located close to the Village of Oak Creek)
- Local Phone: (928) 440-2576

Mariposa Latin Inspired Grill

About:

Mariposa Latin Inspired Grill isn't just a restaurant; it's a fine dining experience nestled amidst the breathtaking red rocks of Sedona, Arizona. Established by Chef Lisa Dahl, Mariposa takes inspiration from her culinary adventures in South America, offering a unique fusion of Latin flavors with an emphasis on fresh, high-quality ingredients.

Food and Ambience:

Prepare to be impressed by both the food and the ambiance at Mariposa. The restaurant features elegant decor with dramatic floor-to-ceiling windows, offering diners panoramic views of Sedona's majestic scenery. The atmosphere is upscale and sophisticated, perfect for a special occasion or a romantic evening.

Cuisine:

Mariposa's cuisine is Latin-inspired, drawing influences from Argentina, Chile, and Uruguay. The menu features delectable dishes showcasing fresh seafood, succulent steaks, and flavorful vegetarian options. You'll also find a curated selection of South American wines to complement your meal.

Price Range:

Mariposa falls into the moderate to high-end price range. Entrees typically range from $30 to $50 or more, with additional costs for appetizers, desserts, and drinks. While it may be a pricier option, the exceptional quality of food, service, and ambiance makes it a worthwhile experience for many.

Location and Contact:

- Address: 700 W Hwy 89A, Sedona, AZ 86336 (Located along Sedona's scenic corridor)
- Website: https://www.mariposasedona.com/
- Phone: (928) 282-9737

Interesting Facts:

- The restaurant itself is a marvel, featuring a 1,000-pound door crafted from African and South American stone, and two glass-enclosed wine vaults showcasing an extensive wine collection.
- Mariposa boasts an on-site herb garden, ensuring fresh ingredients for their delectable dishes.
- The restaurant offers patio seating during the summer months, allowing diners to enjoy their meal under the stars with breathtaking red rock views.
- Reservations are recommended, especially during peak season, due to Mariposa's popularity.

Hideaway House

Nestled amidst the red rocks of Sedona, Hideaway House offers a casual dining experience with a focus on American comfort food and breathtaking scenery.

About:

Hideaway House has been a Sedona staple since the 1950s. Originally a private residence, it transformed into a restaurant, welcoming locals and visitors alike with its charm and relaxed atmosphere.

Food and Ambience:

Embrace the casual vibe at Hideaway House. The restaurant features indoor and patio seating, with the patio offering the most scenic views of Chimney Rock, especially during sunset. Expect friendly service and a welcoming atmosphere where you can unwind and enjoy a satisfying meal.

Cuisine:

Hideaway House serves American comfort food with a Southwestern twist. Think juicy burgers, fresh salads, sandwiches, and classic entrees like steaks and pastas. They also offer a breakfast menu, making it a versatile option for any meal of the day.

Price Range:

Hideaway House falls into the moderate price range. Entrees typically range from $15 to $30, with appetizers, drinks, and desserts adding to the total cost. It's a budget-friendly option for enjoying a good meal in a scenic Sedona location.

Location and Contact:

- Address: 680 Airport Rd, West Sedona, AZ 86336 (Located near the junction of Airport Road and Chimney Rock Road)
- Website: https://sedonahideawayhouse.com/
- Phone: (928) 282-3030

Interesting Facts:

- The history of Hideaway House as a private residence adds to its unique charm.

- The patio seating boasts some of the best views of Chimney Rock in Sedona, making it a popular spot for enjoying a meal with a scenic backdrop.
- They offer live music on certain evenings, adding another layer of entertainment to your dining experience.
- Hideaway House is a dog-friendly restaurant, allowing you to bring your furry friend to enjoy the outdoors on the patio (with proper leash restrictions).

Mesa Grill Sedona

Mesa Grill Sedona beckons diners seeking a delightful blend of delicious comfort food, a relaxed atmosphere, and stunning red rock vistas.

About:

Led by owner and executive chef Mercer Mohr, Mesa Grill Sedona offers a welcoming atmosphere where guests can savor American and Southwestern-inspired cuisine alongside breathtaking Sedona scenery. Whether you're starting your day with breakfast or enjoying a leisurely lunch or dinner, Mesa Grill offers a taste of comfort amidst the beauty of Sedona.

Food and Ambience:

The ambiance at Mesa Grill is both casual and inviting. The restaurant features an indoor dining area and a spacious patio, both offering stunning views of the Sedona Airport Scenic Lookout. Large windows bathe the interior in natural light, creating a warm and comfortable atmosphere. The friendly service adds to the overall relaxed feel.

Cuisine:

Mesa Grill's menu features a delightful mix of American comfort food and Southwestern specialties. Think juicy burgers, fresh salads, perfectly grilled steaks, and flavorful fajitas. They also offer a dedicated breakfast and brunch menu, making it a versatile option for any meal. Inoltre (Italian for "in addition"), they have vegetarian and vegan options to cater to various dietary preferences.

Price Range:

Mesa Grill falls into the mid-range price category. Entrees typically range from $31 to $50, with appetizers, drinks, and desserts adding to the total cost. Considering the quality of the food, the scenic views, and the overall dining experience, it offers good value for your money.

Location and Contact:

- Address: 1185 Airport Rd, Sedona, AZ 86336 (Located right next to the Sedona Airport Scenic Lookout)
- Website: https://mesagrillsedona.com/
- Phone: (928) 282-2400

Interesting Facts:

- Mesa Grill's location is a major perk. Enjoying a delicious meal while gazing out at the red rock vistas creates a memorable dining experience.
- The restaurant features an outdoor viewing deck, offering an even more elevated perspective of the scenery.
- They have a dedicated bar area with a drink menu featuring signature cocktails, local beers, and a selection of wines.
- Mesa Grill is a family-friendly restaurant, offering a kids' menu and high chairs for toddlers.

Dahl & Di Luca Ristorante

Dahl & Di Luca Ristorante is a renowned establishment recognized for setting the standard for Sedona's fine dining scene for over two decades.

About:
Founded by Chef Lisa Dahl, Dahl & Di Luca Ristorante offers an exquisite culinary experience that combines innovative Italian cuisine with fresh, local ingredients. The impeccable service, romantic ambiance, and extensive wine list make it a perfect choice for a special occasion or a memorable evening.

Food and Ambience:
Prepare to be impressed by the elegant atmosphere at Dahl & Di Luca. The intimate setting features warm lighting, crisp linens, and artwork, creating a sophisticated and romantic ambiance. Live jazz piano music adds another layer of sophistication to your dining experience. The attentive and professional service ensures a memorable evening.

Cuisine:
Dahl & Di Luca offers a menu focused on Italian cuisine with a modern twist. Chef Dahl's creativity shines through in her handmade pastas, delectable seafood dishes, and succulent meat entrees. You'll also find vegetarian options to cater to various dietary preferences. Don't forget to explore their impressive wine list, featuring a curated selection of Italian and Californian wines.

Price Range:
Dahl & Di Luca falls into the high-end price range. Entrees typically range from $50 and above, with additional costs for appetizers, desserts, and drinks. While it may be a pricier option, the exceptional quality of the food, service, and ambiance makes it a worthwhile experience for those seeking a fine dining experience in Sedona.

Location and Contact:

- Address: 331 N Main St, Sedona, AZ 86336 (Located in the heart of Uptown Sedona)
- Website: https://www.dahlanddiluca.com/
- Phone: (928) 282-5219

Interesting Facts:

- Chef Lisa Dahl is a James Beard Award-nominated chef, a prestigious recognition in the culinary world.
- The restaurant features a beautiful garden patio, offering a charming outdoor dining option during the warmer months.
- They offer private party options for special occasions, making it a great choice for an unforgettable celebration.
- Reservations are highly recommended, especially during peak season, due to Dahl & Di Luca's popularity.

Creekside American Bistro

Nestled alongside the peaceful Oak Creek in Sedona, Arizona, Creekside American Bistro offers a delightful dining experience that blends comfort food favorites with a warm atmosphere and stunning red rock views.

About:

Established in 2008, Creekside American Bistro has become a favorite amongst locals and visitors alike. Award-winning Chef Mercer Mohr curates a menu that celebrates high-country comfort food, using seasonal and locally-sourced ingredients whenever possible.

Food and Ambience:

The ambiance at Creekside is both welcoming and comfortable. Imagine sinking into a cozy chair and enjoying a delicious meal while surrounded by large windows showcasing the beauty of Sedona's red rocks. The natural light creates a warm and inviting atmosphere, perfect for a relaxed dining experience. During the warmer months, the outdoor patio seating allows diners to soak in the fresh air and breathtaking scenery while enjoying their meal.

Cuisine:

Creekside American Bistro, as the name suggests, focuses on American comfort food with a unique Sedona twist. Their menu features a delightful array of dishes, from juicy steaks and fresh seafood to creative salads, homemade pastas, and decadent desserts. They cater to various dietary preferences with vegetarian and gluten-free options available. Don't forget to explore their brunch menu on weekends, offering a fantastic way to start your day in Sedona.

Price Range:

Creekside falls into the moderate price range. Entrees typically range from $20 to $40, with appetizers, drinks, and desserts adding to the total cost. This makes it a great option for those seeking a delicious and satisfying meal without breaking the bank, especially considering the quality of the food and the beautiful setting.

Location and Contact:

- Address: 251 AZ-179, Sedona, AZ 86336 (Located along the scenic route 179, near Oak Creek Canyon)
- Website: https://creeksidesedona.com/
- Phone: (928) 282-1705

Interesting Facts:

- Creekside American Bistro has won numerous accolades over the years, including being voted "Best Restaurant in Sedona" in 2023.
- The restaurant sources many of its ingredients locally, ensuring fresh and seasonal flavors in their dishes.
- They offer a delightful brunch menu on weekends, featuring breakfast classics with a gourmet touch.
- Creekside is a popular spot for enjoying sunset meals, with the red rocks glowing in the golden light creating a magical backdrop.

Day Trip and Excursion

Grand Canyon National Park

The Grand Canyon National Park, a UNESCO World Heritage Site and one of the Seven Natural Wonders of the World, needs no introduction. Its vastness, colorful layers of rock, and breathtaking vistas leave visitors speechless.

Destination: Grand Canyon National Park, Arizona. There are two main rims of the canyon accessible by car: the South Rim and the North Rim. The South Rim, open year-round, is the more popular choice with various visitor centers, viewpoints, and amenities. The North Rim, at a higher elevation, offers cooler temperatures and a different perspective but has a shorter season (typically mid-May to mid-October).

Activities:

- **Hiking:** The Grand Canyon offers a variety of hiking trails for all skill levels. Popular choices on the South Rim include the South Kaibab Trail for stunning overlooks and the Bright Angel Trail for a more adventurous descent into the canyon. Remember, hiking down into the canyon requires a permit and significant planning due to the strenuous climb back up.
- **Sightseeing:** Multiple viewpoints along the rim offer breathtaking panoramas. Mather Point, Yavapai Point, and Grandview Point are all

excellent choices on the South Rim. For a unique perspective, consider a helicopter tour or a mule ride down into the canyon.

- **Visitor Centers:** The South Rim Visitor Center and the Yavapai Geology Museum offer interactive exhibits and information on the canyon's geology, history, and ecology.

Logistics:

- **Getting There:** The Grand Canyon National Park is located in northern Arizona. The South Rim is easily accessible by car from Phoenix (around a 3.5-hour drive) or Las Vegas (around a 4.5-hour drive). The park also has an airport (Grand Canyon National Park Airport) with limited flight options.
- **Getting Around:** The South Rim has a free shuttle bus system that takes visitors to various viewpoints and visitor centers. Bicycles are also a popular way to get around, and there are designated bike paths.
- **Accommodation:** There are various lodging options within the park, from campgrounds and cabins to lodges and hotels. Reservations, especially during peak season, are highly recommended. Alternatively, consider staying in nearby towns like Tusayan or Williams.

Average Costs:

- **Entrance Fee:** There is a per-vehicle entrance fee to access the National Park. Individual park entrance passes are also av
- taking panoramas. Mather Point, Yavapai Point, and Grandview Point are all excellent choices on the South Rim. For a unique perspective, consider a helicopter tour or a mule ride down into the canyon.
-
- **Visitor Centers:** The South Rim Visitor Center and the Yavapai Geology Museum offer interactive exhibits and information on the canyon's geology, history, and ecology.

Logistics:

- **Getting There:** The Grand Canyon National Park is located in northern Arizona. The South Rim is easily accessible by car from Phoenix (around a 3.5-hour drive) or Las Vegas (around a 4.5-hour drive). The park also has an airport (Grand Canyon National Park Airport) with limited flight options.
- **Getting Around:** The South Rim has a free shuttle bus system that takes visitors to various viewpoints and visitor centers. Bicycles are also a popular way to get around, and there are designated bike paths.
- **Accommodation:** There are various lodging options within the park, from campgrounds and cabins to lodges and hotels. Reservations, especially during peak season, are highly recommended. Alternatively, consider staying in nearby towns like Tusayan or Williams.

Average Costs:

- **Entrance Fee:** There is a per-vehicle entrance fee to access the National Park. Individual park entrance passes are also available.
- **Activities:** Costs for guided tours, mule rides, and helicopter tours vary depending on the chosen option. Hiking is a free activity, but be sure to factor in any permit costs for backcountry camping or overnight hikes.
- **Accommodation:** Lodging options range from budget-friendly campgrounds to luxury hotels. Prices vary depending on the season and type of accommodation.
- **Food:** There are restaurants and concession stands within the park, but expect slightly higher prices compared to outside options. Consider packing a picnic lunch for a budget-friendly alternative.

Tips:

- **Plan Ahead:** The Grand Canyon is a popular destination, especially during peak season (summer and spring). Reserve your accommodation and any necessary permits well in advance.

- **Dress in Layers:** Temperatures can vary significantly depending on the elevation and time of year. Pack layers of clothing and comfortable shoes for any hiking you plan to do.
- **Bring Plenty of Water:** Dehydration is a serious risk at the high altitude of the Grand Canyon. Bring a reusable water bottle and refill it frequently.
- **Respect the Environment:** The Grand Canyon is a fragile ecosystem. Stay on designated trails, pack out all trash, and leave no trace.
- **Be Sun-Safe:** The Arizona sun is strong. Wear sunscreen with a high SPF rating, sunglasses, and a hat to protect yourself from the sun's rays.
- **Consider the North Rim:** If you're looking for a less crowded experience, consider visiting the North Rim. However, keep in mind the shorter operating season and limited amenities compared to the South Rim.

Verde Valley Wine Trail

Arizona isn't just about cacti and canyons. The Verde Valley, nestled between Sedona and Flagstaff, boasts a flourishing wine scene waiting to be explored. The Verde Valley Wine Trail, a scenic route dotted with charming wineries, offers a delightful escape for wine enthusiasts and casual sippers alike.

Destination: The Verde Valley Wine Trail winds through the Verde Valley in Yavapai County, Arizona. Many wineries are located near Cottonwood and surrounding areas, making it an easy day trip from Phoenix (approximately a 1.5-hour drive) or Flagstaff (around a 45-minute drive).

Activities:

- **Wine Tasting:** The heart of the experience lies in indulging in the diverse range of wines produced in the Verde Valley. Each winery offers unique tasting experiences, showcasing their signature varietals and blends. From crisp Viogniers and bold Zinfandels to unique desert wines, there's something for every palate.

-
- **Vineyard Tours:** Many wineries offer guided tours of their vineyards, providing insights into the grape-growing process and the unique terroir of the Verde Valley. Learn about the challenges and triumphs of viticulture in a high-desert environment.

-
- **Culinary Delights:** Pair your wine tasting with delicious food options. Some wineries have on-site restaurants or cafes offering delectable menus that complement the wines. Alternatively, pack a picnic basket and enjoy a scenic lunch amidst the vineyards.
- **Scenic Drives:** The Verde Valley Wine Trail itself is a scenic journey. Wind through rolling hills, past vineyards, and charming towns, soaking in the beauty of the Arizona landscape. Consider taking a detour to explore nearby historic sites or natural wonders like Sedona's red rock formations.

Logistics:

- **Getting There:** The Verde Valley Wine Trail is easily accessible by car. Most wineries offer ample parking for visitors. If you're not comfortable driving after wine tasting, consider hiring a designated driver or using a ride-sharing service.
- **Planning Your Visit:** While some wineries accept walk-in tastings, reservations are recommended, especially during peak season (spring and fall). Check individual winery websites for tasting fees, hours of operation, and any specific reservation requirements.
- **Designated Driver:** It's essential to have a designated driver or plan alternative transportation if you plan on indulging in wine tastings at

multiple wineries. Safety is paramount, and responsible consumption is key to enjoying your experience.

Costs:

- **Tasting Fees:** Tasting fees vary depending on the winery and the selection of wines offered. Expect to pay around $15-$25 per person for a basic tasting. Some wineries might offer premium tasting experiences at higher costs.
- **Food:** Prices for food options at wineries or restaurants along the trail can vary. Consider budgeting for lunch or snacks depending on your preferences.
- **Transportation:** Gas and any potential parking fees are additional considerations.

Tips:

- **Dress Comfortably:** Arizona weather can vary depending on the season. Dress in comfortable clothing and shoes suitable for walking around vineyards and uneven terrain.
- **Bring Sunscreen and Water:** The Arizona sun can be strong, especially during the summer months. Pack sunscreen, sunglasses, and a hat to protect yourself. Don't forget to bring a reusable water bottle and stay hydrated throughout your visit.
- **Responsible Tasting:** Plan your itinerary to allow for responsible consumption. Pace yourself and consider spitting or using a dump bucket if you're trying multiple wines.
- **Embrace the Local Charm:** The Verde Valley Wine Trail is more than just wine. Support local businesses, explore the charming towns along the way, and soak in the unique atmosphere of the region.
- **Extend Your Stay:** Consider turning your wine trail adventure into a multi-day getaway. Explore the surrounding areas, visit historical sites like Montezuma Castle National Monument, or spend time hiking and

enjoying the natural beauty of the Verde Valley.

Events and Festivals

Sedona, nestled amidst the breathtaking red rock formations, comes alive throughout the year with a vibrant calendar of events and festivals.

Some of the major annual gatherings that promise a unique blend of cultural immersion, artistic expression, musical performances, and culinary delights:

January:
Winter Play Day (Typically Held Late January):

- Location: Sedona Bull Ring Park
- This family-friendly event celebrates winter in Sedona with fun activities in the crisp mountain air. Think snow painting, sledding down grassy hills (weather permitting!), arts and crafts, and live entertainment.

February:
Sedona International Film Festival (Typically Held Late February - Early March):

- Location: Various venues throughout Sedona
- Movie buffs rejoice! This prestigious film festival showcases independent, international, and documentary films across various genres. Expect red carpet galas, filmmaker Q&A sessions, and screenings in iconic locations like Sedona's natural amphitheaters.

March:
Sedona Mountain Bike Festival (Typically Held Early March):

- Location: Bell Rock Pathway
- Calling all cycling enthusiasts! This three-day festival offers a range of mountain bike races, clinics, demos, and gear expos for all skill levels. Enjoy the camaraderie of fellow cyclists amidst Sedona's stunning scenery.

Celebration of Spring (Typically Held Mid-March):

- Location: Tlaquepaque Arts & Shopping Village
- Welcome spring with this lively event at the charming Tlaquepaque Arts & Shopping Village. Expect live music, art demonstrations, cultural performances, and special shopping promotions.

April:
Sedona St. Patrick's Day Parade (March 17th):

- Location: Uptown Sedona
- Don your green attire and join the festive spirit of Sedona's St. Patrick's Day parade. This lively procession features marching bands, floats, and local businesses showcasing their Irish spirit.

Sedona Hummingbird Festival (Typically Held Mid-April to Early May):

- Location: Various locations throughout Sedona
- Celebrate the arrival of these fascinating creatures at the Sedona Hummingbird Festival. Embark on guided hikes to see hummingbirds in their natural habitat, attend informative lectures, and participate in family-friendly activities.

May:

Red Dirt Music Festival (Typically Held Early May & Late September):

- Location: Poco Diablo Ranch
- Immerse yourself in the twangy sounds of Texas Country music at the Red Dirt Music Festival. This two-day event features renowned and rising stars of the Red Dirt music scene, creating an unforgettable atmosphere under the Sedona sky.

June:

Cinema Series (Throughout June):

- Location: Sedona Viewpoint
- Enjoy classic and cult-favorite films under the stars at the Sedona Viewpoint with the Cinema Series. Pack a picnic basket, cozy up under the blankets, and enjoy a unique movie night amidst the red rocks.

July:

4th of July Wet Fest (July 4th):

- Location: Slide Rock State Park
- Beat the summer heat with a splashtastic time at Slide Rock State Park's 4th of July Wet Fest. This family-friendly event features water slides, games, and live music, culminating in a spectacular fireworks display over Chimney Rock.

September:

- **Red Dirt Music Festival (Typically Held Early May & Late September)**

October:
Sedona Arts Festival (Typically Held Mid-October):

- Location: Uptown Sedona
- Art lovers rejoice! The Sedona Arts Festival is a premier event showcasing the works of over 100 juried artists from across the country. Explore a wide range of artistic mediums, including paintings, sculptures, jewelry, and ceramics, all displayed against the backdrop of Sedona's red rocks.

The Great Pumpkin Splash (Typically Held Late October):

- Location: Slide Rock State Park
- A quirky and fun event for families, the Great Pumpkin Splash encourages participants to race decorated pumpkins down the natural water slides at Slide

Must Visit Farmer's Market

Sedona Community Farmers Market (Typically Sundays, Late Fall - Early Spring):

- **Location:** Well Fargo Bank Parking Lot (West Sedona)
- **Best Time to Visit:** Enjoy the sunshine and fresh air with a visit on Sundays between 11 am and 3 pm during the operational season.
- **Offerings:** This farmers market champions local agriculture and sustainability. Expect a bounty of locally-grown fruits and vegetables, farm-fresh eggs and dairy products, artisan breads, and locally-produced honey. You might also find locally-raised meats and handcrafted soaps and bath products made with natural ingredients.
- **Special Features:** The market often features live music, creating a lively atmosphere while you shop.

Tlaquepaque Arts & Shopping Village:

- **Location:** Throughout Tlaquepaque Arts & Shopping Village
- **Best Time to Visit:** Open year-round, this charming village transforms into a vibrant marketplace on special occasions. Check their event calendar for specific dates.
- **Offerings:** Think of it as an ongoing art and cultural fair. Explore over 50 specialty shops and galleries showcasing a diverse range of artwork, handcrafted jewelry, pottery, and home décor items, all reflecting the artistic spirit of the Southwest. Witness local artisans demonstrating their craft in some galleries, adding an interactive element to your shopping experience.
- **Special Features:** Tlaquepaque often hosts special events throughout the year, like "Second Saturdays" featuring artist meet-and-greets and live music.

Sedona Film Festival Street Fair (Typically Held During Sedona International Film Festival - Late February/Early March):

- **Location:** Uptown Sedona
- **Best Time to Visit:** This street fair coincides with the Sedona International Film Festival, so plan your visit during the festival dates.
- **Offerings:** Immerse yourself in the world of cinema! This street fair features booths with film festival merchandise, movie-themed games and activities, and live entertainment.
- **Special Features:** Mingle with fellow movie enthusiasts, enjoy festival food trucks, and potentially catch a glimpse of some of the filmmakers attending the festival.

Holiday Shopping Events:

- **Locations:** Uptown Sedona, Tlaquepaque
- **Best Time to Visit:** During the holiday season (Thanksgiving through

New Year's), Sedona transforms into a winter wonderland with festive lighting and special shopping events.

- **Offerings:** Uptown Sedona and Tlaquepaque often host holiday-themed markets with local vendors selling unique gifts, handcrafted ornaments, seasonal treats, and festive décor.
- **Special Features:** Enjoy carolers spreading holiday cheer, carriage rides through the streets, and special holiday menus at Sedona's restaurants.

Additional Tips:

- **Weather:** Keep Sedona's weather in mind when planning your visit to outdoor markets. Opt for the cooler morning hours during summer and enjoy the sunshine in the afternoons during the cooler months.
- **Cash & Cards:** While most vendors accept credit cards, it's always a good idea to carry some cash for smaller purchases at local markets.
- **Support Local:** Sedona thrives on its local artisans and farmers. Take home a unique piece of Sedona by shopping at these markets and fairs.

Itinerary

Escape to Sedona: A Romantic Weekend Itinerary

Sedona, enveloped by captivating red rock formations and brimming with artistic energy, offers the perfect backdrop for a romantic escape.

Day 1: Arrival and Setting the Mood

- **Morning:**Check into your luxurious accommodations. Consider options like the enchanting **L'Auberge de Sedona** with its creekside setting and fireplaces in some rooms, or the **Sedona Penthouse** boasting breathtaking red rock views from a private balcony.
-
- **Afternoon:**Embark on a scenic stroll hand-in-hand through **West Fork Trail**. This moderate trail offers captivating views of Chimney Rock and Coffee Pot Rock, perfect for capturing those romantic Instagram-worthy moments.
- **Early Evening:**Indulge in an intimate couples massage at the renowned **Mii Amo Spa**. Surrounded by the tranquility of the red rocks, this spa experience will melt away stress and set the mood for a romantic getaway.
- **Evening:**Savor a delectable dinner at **Couples Canyon at The Collective**. This open-air restaurant nestled amidst the red rocks provides an enchanting ambiance, and the menu features locally-sourced ingredients with a focus on seasonal flavors. Enjoy creative dishes like juniper-

dusted duck breast or mesquite-grilled filet mignon, complemented by an extensive wine list.

Day 2: Unveiling the Beauty of Sedona

- **Morning:**Fuel up for a day of exploration with a delicious breakfast at **Hideout Coffee House**. This cozy cafe offers a warm and inviting atmosphere, perfect for enjoying pastries and handcrafted coffee creations.
- **Mid-Morning:**Immerse yourselves in the beauty and history of Sedona at **The Palatki Ruins**. This archeological site, featuring cliff dwellings nestled amidst the red rocks, offers a glimpse into the lives of the Sinagua people who inhabited the area centuries ago. Embark on a guided tour to learn more about the history and culture of this fascinating civilization.
- **Afternoon:**Pack a picnic basket with gourmet cheeses, local fruits, and crusty bread, and head to **Bell Rock Pathway** for a scenic hike. This easy-to-moderate trail circumnavigates the iconic Bell Rock formation, offering stunning views and plenty of opportunities for capturing romantic moments.
- **Evening:**Witness a breathtaking sunset over Sedona's red rocks from **Schnebly Hill**. This scenic overlook provides a panoramic vista, perfect for a romantic embrace as the sky explodes with vibrant colors.
- **Night:**Enjoy an intimate fine-dining experience at **Restaurant Row** in Uptown Sedona. Choose from a variety of acclaimed restaurants, each offering a unique ambiance and culinary delights. For an unparalleled experience, consider **Matisse** ( ) where French-inspired cuisine meets stunning red rock views.

Day 3: Cultural Delights and Farewell

- **Morning:**Explore the vibrant art scene of Sedona with a stroll through the galleries in **Uptown Sedona** and **Tlaquepaque Arts & Shopping Village**. Discover paintings, sculptures, and handcrafted jewelry created by local artists, and take home a unique piece of Sedona as a memento of your romantic getaway.

- **Afternoon:**Immerse yourselves in the energy vortexes believed to exist in Sedona. Embark on a guided vortex tour or explore some of the popular vortex sites like **Airport Mesa** or **Cathedral Rock**. Whether you're a believer or not, the serene beauty of these locations is sure to leave a lasting impression.
- **Early Evening:**Savor a final romantic dinner at **Oak Creek Canyon Grille**. This restaurant, nestled amidst the lush greenery of Oak Creek Canyon, offers a delightful ambiance and a menu featuring innovative dishes prepared with fresh, seasonal ingredients.

A 5-Day Family Adventure Itinerary

Sedona isn't just for couples seeking romance! This captivating destination offers a treasure trove of adventures for families.

Day 1: Arrival and Setting the Stage for Adventure

- **Morning:** Check into your comfortable and spacious accommodations. Consider options like **The Sedona We Care Vacation Rentals** with multiple bedrooms and potentially a pool, or **Verde Valley Haciendas Resort** featuring kid-friendly amenities like a pool and playground.
- **Afternoon:** Head to **Slide Rock State Park** for a splashtastic afternoon. This natural water slide carved by millennia of water flow provides endless fun for kids of all ages. Pack swimsuits, towels, and water shoes for a safe and enjoyable experience.
- **Evening:** Enjoy a casual family dinner at **The Hideaway House**. This restaurant caters to families with a kid-friendly menu featuring pizzas, burgers, and pasta dishes. The outdoor patio offers a relaxed atmosphere perfect for unwinding after a day of adventure.

Day 2: Exploring the Wonders of the Red Rocks

- **Morning:**Embark on a family-friendly hike on the **Fay Canyon Trail**. This easy-to-moderate trail offers breathtaking views of the red rock formations and plenty of opportunities for spotting wildlife. Look out for lizards, snakes (keep a safe distance!), and various bird species.
- **Afternoon:**Visit the **Sedona Heritage Museum**. This interactive museum brings Sedona's history and culture to life with educational exhibits and activities geared towards children. Kids can learn about the Sinagua people who once inhabited the area, explore dioramas depicting the region's diverse ecosystems, and participate in hands-on activities like pottery making (check for specific schedules).
- **Evening:**Enjoy a delicious and family-friendly dinner at **Creekside Pizza Company**. They offer a variety of pizzas with unique topping combinations, along with pasta dishes and salads to satisfy everyone's appetite. The lively atmosphere adds to the fun dining experience.

Day 3: Jeep Tour and Off-Road Adventure

- **Morning:** Embark on a thrilling jeep tour through the red rocks. Many companies offer family-friendly tours with knowledgeable guides who will point out interesting rock formations, share fascinating facts about Sedona's geology and history, and keep the adventure engaging for all ages. Choose a tour that caters to your comfort level - some offer scenic explorations, while others might have more adventurous off-roading elements.
- **Afternoon:** Visit **Jimmie's T-Rex Grill** for a break after the jeep tour. This restaurant offers dinosaur-themed décor alongside a casual dining experience. Kids will love the burgers and fries, while adults can enjoy sandwiches and salads.
- **Evening:** Attend a stargazing session at **Dark Sky Tours**. Sedona boasts minimal light pollution, making it a prime location for stargazing.

These tours, often held after sunset, provide telescopes and expert guidance to help families explore the wonders of the night sky. Learn about constellations, planets, and the Milky Way, creating a memorable experience for all.

Day 4: Artistic Expression and Cultural Immersion

Morning:

- Take a family art class at **The Art Barn**. This studio offers workshops and classes designed specifically for families. Kids can unleash their creativity with painting, pottery, or jewelry making, all under the guidance of experienced instructors.

Afternoon:

- Explore the vibrant art scene of **Tlaquepaque Arts & Shopping Village**. This charming village features over 50 galleries and shops showcasing local artwork, handcrafted items, and souvenirs. Kids will enjoy browsing the colorful displays and spotting unique creations.

Evening:

- Savor a delicious dinner with a focus on Native American cuisine at **Chocolatree**. This restaurant offers a unique dining experience where traditional dishes are reinterpreted with a modern twist. The menu features items like blue corn enchiladas, slow-roasted turkey, and fresh

Day 5: Farewell to Sedona and Lasting Memories

- **Morning:**Enjoy a leisurely breakfast at your accommodations or grab pastries and coffee from a local cafe like **Coffee Pot Restaurant**. This family-friendly diner offers classic breakfast fare like pancakes, waffles, and omelets in a casual setting.
- **Mid-Morning:**Embark on a scenic drive through **Oak Creek Canyon**. This stunning canyon, nicknamed the "Grand Canyon's little sister," offers breathtaking views and a variety of pull-off points for photo opportunities and short hikes. Keep an eye out for deer, hawks, and other wildlife along the way.
- **Afternoon:**Spend some time at **Slide Rock State Park** again (if permitted by your departure schedule) or explore another kid-friendly option like **Red Rock Crossing**. This scenic location features a shallow creek perfect for wading and splashing, with towering red rock formations providing a dramatic backdrop.

Tips:

- **Beat the Heat:** Sedona's summers can be scorching. Plan strenuous activities like hiking for the cooler morning hours, and opt for water-based activities or indoor attractions during the afternoon heat.
- **Sunscreen & Hydration:** Sunscreen is a must-have, especially for children. Bring plenty of water to stay hydrated throughout your adventures.
- **Picnics:** Pack lunches for park visits to save time and money.

Consider a Sedona Red Rock Visitor Center Pass: If you plan on visiting multiple parks and museums throughout your stay, purchasing a Sedona Red Rock Visitor Center Pass can save you money on entrance fees.

7-Day Adventure for Outdoor Enthusiasts, History Buffs, and Foodies

Sedona beckons with its fiery red rocks, rich history, and diverse culinary scene. This 7-day itinerary blends outdoor adventures, cultural immersion, and delectable dining experiences, crafting an unforgettable escape for outdoor enthusiasts, history buffs, and foodies alike.

Day 1: Embrace the Red Rocks

- **Morning:** Check into your comfortable accommodations. Consider options near Uptown Sedona or West Sedona for easy access to hiking trails and restaurants.
- **Afternoon:** Embark on a scenic hike on **West Fork Trail**. This moderate trail offers breathtaking views of Chimney Rock and Coffee Pot Rock formations, perfect for igniting your sense of adventure. Keep an eye out for diverse birdlife and unique desert flora.
- **Evening:** Savor a delicious welcome dinner at **Elote Cafe**. This lively restaurant offers modern takes on classic Mexican cuisine, featuring fresh, locally-sourced ingredients and a vibrant atmosphere. Enjoy handcrafted margaritas and indulge in dishes like wood-fired carne asada or flavorful mole poblano.

Day 2: Unveiling Sedona's Past

Morning:

Immerse yourself in the history of the Sinagua people at **Palatki Ruins**. This archeological site, featuring cliff dwellings nestled amidst the red rocks, offers a glimpse into the lives of this ancient civilization. Embark on a guided tour to learn about their culture, architecture, and way of life.

Afternoon:

Experience the power of nature with a **Jeep Tour** through the backcountry. Explore hidden canyons, ancient petroglyphs (rock art), and witness the vastness of Sedona's wilderness. Choose a tour that caters to your interests, ranging from scenic explorations to more adventurous off-roading experiences.

Evening:

Feast on a hearty dinner at **The Cowboy Club**. This restaurant, steeped in Western history, offers a unique ambiance and classic American cuisine. Dig into juicy steaks, succulent ribs, or opt for lighter options like fresh fish or pasta dishes.

Day 3: A Culinary Journey and Artistic Inspiration

- **Morning:** Fuel up for the day with a delicious breakfast at **Wildflower Bakery**. This bakery offers a delightful selection of pastries, breads, and breakfast sandwiches made with fresh, high-quality ingredients. Savor their famous sticky buns or indulge in a savory quiche.
- **Mid-Morning:** Explore the vibrant art scene of **Uptown Sedona**. Stroll through galleries showcasing the works of local and regional artists, and discover a variety of artistic mediums like paintings, sculptures, and jewelry. Take home a unique piece of Sedona as a memento of your trip.
- **Afternoon:** Treat your taste buds to a gourmet picnic lunch at **The Secret Garden Cafe**. This charming cafe offers a delightful selection of salads, sandwiches, and wraps made with fresh, seasonal ingredients. Pick up a picnic basket and head to a scenic spot like **Bell Rock Pathway** to enjoy your meal amidst the red rocks.

Day 4: Conquering the Landscape

- **Morning:** Challenge yourself with a hike on **Cathedral Rock Trail**. This strenuous hike offers breathtaking panoramic views of Sedona, rewarding you for your effort. Be sure to wear proper hiking shoes and bring plenty of water for this challenging but rewarding adventure.

- **Afternoon:** Relax and rejuvenate your muscles with a therapeutic massage at the renowned **Mii Amo Spa**. Surrounded by the tranquility of the red rocks, this spa experience will melt away stress and allow you to fully immerse yourself in the beauty of Sedona.
- **Evening:** Indulge in a luxurious dining experience at **Matisse**. This acclaimed restaurant offers French-inspired cuisine with an emphasis on fresh, seasonal ingredients and stunning red rock views. Savor delectable dishes paired with an extensive wine list for a truly unforgettable evening.

Day 5: Unveiling the Power of Water

- **Morning:** Embark on a kayak tour down the Verde River. This scenic adventure allows you to explore Sedona's natural beauty from a unique perspective. Witness towering red rock formations from the water, spot diverse birdlife, and enjoy a peaceful float down the river.
- **Afternoon:** Visit **Montezuma Castle National Monument**. This cliff dwelling, nestled high in the canyon walls, offers a glimpse into the lives of the Sinagua people

Day 6: A Day for Reflection and Exploration

- **Morning:** Enjoy a leisurely breakfast at your accommodations or grab a coffee and pastry from a local cafe like **Coffee Pot Restaurant**. This family-friendly diner offers classic breakfast fare in a casual setting.
- **Mid-Morning:** Embark on a self-guided exploration of **Schnebly Hill**. This scenic overlook offers breathtaking panoramic views of Sedona, particularly captivating during sunrise or sunset. Take in the vastness of the landscape and find a quiet spot for meditation or reflection.
- **Afternoon:** Explore the diverse offerings at **Tlaquepaque Arts &**

Shopping Village. This charming village features over 50 galleries and shops showcasing local artwork, handcrafted items, and souvenirs. Browse through the vibrant displays, and perhaps treat yourself to a unique piece of jewelry or a hand-painted ceramic memento.

- **Evening:** Savor a farewell dinner at **Oak Creek Canyon Grille**. Nestled amidst the lush greenery of Oak Creek Canyon, this restaurant offers a delightful ambiance and a menu featuring innovative dishes prepared with fresh, seasonal ingredients. Enjoy panoramic views of the canyon while indulging in creative takes on classic dishes like steaks, seafood, or pastas.

Day 7: Departure with Memories to Last a Lifetime

- **Morning:** Enjoy a final breakfast at your accommodations or explore the local farmers market (depending on the day of the week) for fresh produce and artisan products.
- **Afternoon:** Depending on your departure time, you can squeeze in some last-minute souvenir shopping at local stores in Uptown Sedona or West Sedona.
- **Late Afternoon:** Bid farewell to Sedona, carrying cherished memories of outdoor adventures, historical discoveries, and culinary delights.

Conclusion

Sedona's magic transcends its fiery red rocks. It's a place where adventure ignites, history whispers secrets, and culinary creations tantalize the taste buds. This comprehensive guide has equipped you with the tools to craft your own unforgettable Sedona experience.

Whether you crave adrenaline-pumping hikes, delve into the past, or savor the vibrant flavors of the region, Sedona has something for everyone. So, lace up your boots, pack your curiosity, and embark on a journey that will leave you breathless, inspired, and yearning to return to this captivating land. Remember, Sedona's magic lies not just in the sights and experiences, but in the way it touches your soul.

Embrace the adventure, and let Sedona weave its spell on you.

14631466R00075